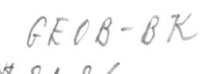

BUSINESS REFERENCE GUIDE

CONCEPTS IN FINANCE

The Editors of Salem Press

SALEM PRESS
A Division of EBSCO Information Services
Ipswich, Massachusetts

Copyright ©2014, by Salem Press, A Division of EBSCO Information Services, Inc.

All rights reserved. No part of this work may be used or reproduced in any manner whatsoever or transmitted in any form or by any means, electronic or mechanical, including photocopy, recording, or any information storage and retrieval system, without written permission from the copyright owner. For permissions requests, contact proprietarypublishing@ebscohost.com.

ISBN: 978-0-8242-1399-2

ebook: 978-1-4298-3558-9

Contents

Introduction	v
Basic Concepts in Finance	1
National Elections & Business Cycles	7
Capital Budgeting	13
Financial Management in Business	18
Use of Managerial Economics in Finance	24
Financial Information Systems	30
Managerial Finance	36
Strategic Financial Management	42
Financing the Corporation	48
Financial Incentives	55
Cash Flow	61
Terminal Value	68
Debt Valuation	74
Warrants & Convertibles	80
Swaps	86

Introduction

An understanding of money and economics is not only important in managing personal finances, but also in managing corporations and nonprofits. Without knowledge of the fundamentals, managers would be unable to structure and build their organization for future financial growth and strategic plan implementation.

The *Business Reference Guide* series is designed to provide a solid foundation for the research of various business topics. This volume offers an expansive overview of general concepts in finance, including budgeting, managerial finance, and financial theory.

The essay collection begins with an article on the primary elements of finance. Among the topics covered are the time value of money, asset valuation, risk management, and financial planning. Marie Gould applies the topic of finance to the corporate and nonprofit sectors, and she stresses the importance of having organizations create strategic plans and analyze all financial records in order to foster growth and turn profits. Gould also introduces the concept of capital budgeting, which is further developed by Sue Ann Connaughton, who maintains that "capital budgeting is the procedure [used] for establishing whether or not a company should invest in projects such as new facilities or products." Nancy Devenger furthers the corporate and nonprofit discussion by delivering an overview of financial management in business. Devenger continues with an overview of the ever-changing role of financial managers, who are recognized for their importance in determining whether or not a company is able to meet its goals and objectives. In order to reach these goals, it is necessary for companies to make decisions based on financial and economic analysis. Gould returns with an outline of some of the decisions that managers make and an overview of the importance of financial accounting and information systems. Other specific decisions that corporate managers may make, as outlined by Marlanda English, often involve dividend policy, capital spending, and the funding of long- and short-term projects. Another issue often confronted by financial managers and organizations is financing; to tackle financing, Gould outlines debt and capital equity, which serve as the two primary financing methods. Ruth A. Wienclaw also details a variety of government-provided financial incentives, some of which help in the development of small businesses.

The remaining essays in this collection cover a variety of topics that are often discussed in relation to finance. The first of these, written by Carolyn Sprague, describes the importance of effective cash flow management and the difficulties associated with maintaining a steady influx of cash assets. Sprague also defines terminal value as the overall worth of an organization, which can be determined through three methods: liquidation values, exit multiples, and the stable growth model. In order to estimate an organization's value, one must also conduct debt valuation. Sprague offers an interesting essay that encompasses the benefits of incurring debt to spur growth and the pitfalls of maintaining unstable levels of debt. She also sheds light on the roles that private equity firms and leveraged buyouts play on the increasing amounts of corporate debt. Devenger and Gould conclude the volume with an overview of the different financial investment vehicles, including warrants and convertibles, and a detailed account of interest rate swaps.

The fundamental concepts of finance continue to play an integral role in the structuring of organizations for future growth and stability. This volume will allow readers to consider ad study the general concepts of finance. Complete bibliographic entries, a list of suggested readings, and relevant terms and concepts finish the essay.

Basic Concepts in Finance

Table of Contents

Abstract

Overview

    Decreased Savings & Increased Debt

Applications

    Successful Saving

    Instruments for Saving

    Certificates of Deposit

    Money-Market Deposit Account

    Money Market Mutual Fund

    Benefits of Savings Instruments

    Interest Accrual

    Real Estate

    Stocks, Bonds & Mutual Funds

    Time Value of Money

    Interest Calculations

    Asset Valuation

    Risk Assessment

Viewpoints

Terms & Concepts

Bibliography

Suggested Reading

Abstract

This article concerns finance, that is, the study of how resources are valued, allocated and invested over time. Having knowledge of the basic concepts of finance is important not only for business owners, corporate executives and financial planners; ultimately, financial planning is each individual's responsibility. Three of the most fundamental concepts in finance are the time value of money, asset valuation, that is, how the value of stocks, bonds, real estate, and other investments is determined, and finally, risk management. While the time value of money is the basis for the other concepts, financial planning and investing ultimately require an understanding of risk management. This article will approach the basic concepts of finance for the individual and provide an overview of financial and investment products.

Overview

It is becoming increasingly important for individuals to assume responsibility for planning a financial future. Successful financial planning, in turn, requires one to understand the basic concepts of finance since this understanding will afford one the ability to save and invest wisely. This means that the individual needs to have knowledge of a variety of financial products and investments and comprehend how these vehicles work. Moreover, for many people, the largest investment they will make is purchasing a home. Having knowledge of the basic concepts of finance will enable them to understand mortgages and consumer debt in general. Saving, other investments and managing debt are all based upon the foundation of the first financial concept — the time value of money. Further, this concept is a building block to asset valuation and risk management. Asset valuation requires one to understand how the value of assets such as stocks, bonds and real estate are determined. Finally, understanding such concepts as compound interest and inflation can empower an individual to manage the risk of their investments over time.

Decreased Savings & Increased Debt

However, recent research indicates that many people are financially illiterate — they do not have an understanding of the basic concepts of finance. People cannot differentiate between individual stocks and stock mutual funds, nor do they comprehend that investing in individual stocks is riskier than investing in mutual funds. Further, there is a general lack of knowledge about compound interest and inflation. This lack of knowledge reflects the fact that many people do not understand how money works, and this in turn is manifested in the way people invest or fail to invest their money. For many, their primary investment vehicle is their company provided defined benefit plan or a defined contribution plan. A defined benefit plan is commonly referred to as a fully funded pension. However, pension plans are becoming less common as employers are shifting this benefit to a defined contribution plan such as a 401(k). Unfortunately, many people are not aware of the differences between these two types of plans and some are not certain which type of plan their employer provides. The result of this lack of knowledge is that the overall savings rate declined dramatically during the late twentieth and early twenty-first centuries (Carlson, 2005), and only started to rise in the wake of the 2007 recession (Samavati, Adilov, & Dilts, 2013).

More importantly, the amount of consumer debt dramatically increased as the twentieth century came to a close. This is reflected by the fact that more people carried higher amounts of unsecured consumer debt such as credit cards. This trend, as is the case with the overall savings rate, has slightly reversed since the 2007 recession (Brown, Haughwout, Donghoon, & van der Klaauw, 2013). In addition to an expansion of unsecured debt, the rise in home ownership over the last 20 years combined with the rising value of real property has resulted in a surge of mortgage debt. In order for the individual to be able to adequately finance this debt requires an understanding of the basic concepts of finance.

Applications

Successful Saving

While having an understanding of the basic concepts of finance is important to understanding the value of savings and investing, saving is really a matter of common sense money management. In this regard, there are four ways to simply start saving.

- First, large amounts of cash should not be kept on hand, but rather deposited into a savings account.
- Second, although paying outstanding bills on time is important, there is no benefit derived from paying bills early and this money can continue to earn interest.
- Further, some people intentionally have more taxes withheld in order to obtain a refund. However, that excess money could also be put to better use by earning interest.
- Finally, once the amount of money a person is saving begins to accumulate, it can then be invested in other ways to earn even more interest such as by opening an interest bearing checking account (Miller, 2003).

Instruments for Saving
Certificates of Deposit

Another vehicle available for savings investment is a Certificate of Deposit or a CD. Investing in a CD is essentially a time-deposit savings device that requires an investor to keep the money in the account for a specified period of time. That period can be for as little as 3-6 months or as long as 5 years. In return for this, the interest rate paid by the bank is higher than the interest rates based on savings accounts or interest bearing checking accounts. The longer the term of the CD, the higher the interest rate that will be paid. In addition, there is usually a penalty for withdrawing the money early.

Money-Market Deposit Account

Another type of savings account available for basic investing is a Money-Market Deposit Account (MMDA). This is basically a means of saving that is a cross between a savings account and a Certificate of Deposit. An MMDA requires an investor to maintain a minimum balance ($1,000) while allowing for a maximum number of three checks to be drawn each month (but automated deposit machine withdrawals are not limited).

Money Market Mutual Fund

In addition to the MMDA, an individual can also invest in a Money Market Mutual Fund. Opening this type of fund requires a minimum initial deposit, usually $1,000, $5,000 or more depending on the financial institution. The institution uses the money invested in these funds to borrow and lend money on a short-term basis. This includes such investment vehicles as commercial paper (short-term debt obligations issued by a corporation), Treasury bills (short term debt issued by the Federal government), federal government securities such as "Ginnie Maes" (GNMAs) and "Fannie Maes (FNMAs) as well as others short term debt instruments (Miller, 2003).

Benefits of Savings Instruments

The main benefit of the foregoing savings instruments is that they allow an investor to earn interest on their money without a great deal of risk. The general rule of thumb regarding saving money is that one should have six months of living expenses set aside. This is not money to spend or to be used for making large purchases and should only be used in case of an emergency or loss of income. Having this money set aside will also enable an individual to minimize their debts. As mentioned earlier, not saving enough money is one of the biggest financial mistakes that people make. Another way to save money is to open an Individual Retirement Account (IRA) or contribute to an employer sponsored plan such as a 401(k). Investing in these instruments enables an individual to invest in stocks, bonds, mutual funds, certificates of deposit, money-market funds, and the like (Chatzky, 2004).

Interest Accrual

In addition to understanding financial concepts that are at the root of all these investments, it is also helpful to comprehend the goal of investing, and the benefits of investing in stocks, bonds, mutual funds, and even real estate. An investment is basically the use of money for the purpose of creating more money. This can be accomplished by putting money in income-producing vehicles, such as the various savings vehicles that earn interest mentioned above. Interest is essentially the cost of using money, usually over a one-year period and an interest rate is the rate charged for using that money. For example, if a bank was offering an interest rate of 2% per year on a basic savings account, and an initial deposit of $1,000 is made, after one year, that account would have $1,020 On the other hand, interest rates are charged on bonds, credit cards, and other types of consumer and business loans. If a bank charges $600 per year on a loan of $100,000, the interest rate would be 6% per year (Downes, 2006).

Real Estate

Interest rates on consumer loans are important to understand if a person is buying a home. Financing an investment in real estate usually requires obtaining a mortgage from a financial institution. A mortgage is a debt instrument a lender uses to place a lien on real property purchased by the borrower. A lien is a creditor's claim, in this case the lender, against property (Downes, 2006). By understanding the time value of money, a person will be better able to understand how much a mortgage will actually cost over 30 years. By understanding asset valuation, a person can determine the value of the house, or the asset. An asset, moreover, is anything with financial value that is owned by a business or person.

Stocks, Bonds & Mutual Funds

In addition to an asset such as real estate, an individual can also invest in stocks, bonds, and mutual funds. Investing in stock essentially means to have an ownership interest in a corporation. Shares issued by the corporation represent stock ownership, and these are claims against a company's earnings and assets. The value of stock is determined by a number of factors over time. On the other hand, an individual can also invest in bonds. Basically, a bond is an interest-bearing government or corporate instrument that requires the issuer to pay specific amounts of money at certain time intervals until the debt is paid in full by a set date (also referred to as the maturity date). Another way to invest in stocks and bonds is to invest in a mutual fund. A mutual fund is an investment vehicle that is operated by an investment company. Money is raised from shareholders, and that money is used to invest in stocks, bonds, and other investments (Downes, 2006). The benefit of investing in mutual funds is that the investment company manages the risk.

For many people, one convenient way to invest in stocks, bonds and mutual funds is to participate in an employer-sponsored savings and retirement plan like a 401(k) or 403(b) plan. These plans are also called defined contribution plans. In a 401(k), the plan is managed by an investment company and requires the employee to contribute a percentage of their income. In some cases, the employer also contributes to the plan, and this is referred to as a company match. The company match usually equates to 50% of the employee's contribution. For example, an employee that contributes 6% of their income to a 401(k) will see the company make a matching contribution of 3%. In short, this means that a person will be saving and investing 9% of their annual income by participating in such a plan (Carlson, 2005).

For those that do not have access to a 401(k), another way to invest in mutual funds is to invest in an individual retirement account, also known as an IRA (Fryar, Warther, Thibodeau, & Drucker, 2012). There are different types of individual retirement accounts. A traditional IRA is one where an individual makes tax deferred payments. A Roth IRA, on the other hand, enables an investor to contribute money that has already been taxed. Of course, there are many other factors and considerations in regard to IRAs, but investing in these retirement vehicles require an individual to take responsibility for their financial planning. Regardless of the types of investment a person makes, having an understanding of the basic concepts of finance can be helpful. While the fundamental concepts of finance might be considered basic, they can also be complicated. This is so because understanding these concepts requires determining the time value of money, asset valuation and risk management.

Time Value of Money

The first and foremost principle in finance is the time value of money because financial decisions are spread out over time. This concept essentially is a means of calculating the value of a sum of money in the present or in the future. While the outcome of financial decisions cannot be known with certainty, being able to calculate the value of money at some time in the future affords one the ability to manage risk. Understanding the time value of money allows one to calculate present and future values. In the parlance of financial planning present value or "PV" means the present value of an amount that will be received in the future. On the other hand, future value or "FV" is the future worth of a present amount. For example, understanding PV will enable a bond investor to determine the value now of a $1,000 bond that will mature in ten years. On the other hand, FV will enable an individual to determine how much a $1,000 savings account will have at the end of the year if it pays 2% interest compounded annually (Clare, 2002).

Interest Calculations

With respect to interest, there are fundamentally two ways to calculate it — simple interest and compound interest.

- Simple Interest is a calculation based only on the original principal amount of the asset or debt. For instance, in the example mentioned above, a $1,000 deposit in a savings account at 2% simple interest would earn $20 per year (2% of $1,000 = $20). At the end of the first year, the amount of the principal and interest in the account would equate to $1,020.

- On the other hand, compound interest is interest earned on the principal plus any interest that was previously earned. For example, a $1,000 deposit at 5% compound interest at the end of the first year would earn $50 in the first year (5% of $1,000 = $50). If no additional deposits are made in the second year the balance in the account would be $1,102.50 or 5% of $1,050 = $52.50; $1,050 + $52.50 = $1,102.50 (Downes, 2006).

Asset Valuation

In addition to understanding the basics of time value, and being able to calculate interest, it is also necessary to understand how assets are valued. The value of an asset, in turn, is partially determined by the market where the asset is bought and sold. With respect to stocks, asset value is determined by the net value of a company's assets on a per share basis as opposed to the shares' market value (Downes, 2006). One of the key ingredients in determining this value is how profitable the company is in a given period of time. In a real estate transaction, the value of real property is determined by an appraisal of the property and there are numerous factors to consider such as the type of property, the number of units in the dwelling, the location and condition of the real property and the value of other properties in the vicinity. The importance of understanding asset valuation as it relates to the property is also an important consideration in determining the loan amount of the mortgage that a financial institution will offer to a purchaser.

Risk Assessment

The last concept that an investor needs to consider is risk or the potential for the loss of value of an asset. One such way to manage risks is to value assets by using comparative scenarios that consider a range of assumptions (Clare, 2002). Some of the specific considerations in this regard are inflation risk, interest rate risk, credit risk and risk of principal. Inflation risk is the potential that the value of an asset or income will erode as increased prices adversely affect the value of money. Interest rate risk is the possibility that a fixed rate debt instrument will decline in value as interest rates rise. Credit risk is the possibility that a debtor will not repay an obligation. Finally, risk of principal is the chance that money that was initially invested will lose its value. In short, risk management requires one to have knowledge of the asset in which they are investing as well as knowledge of various market and economic conditions affecting that market.

Viewpoints

In the final analysis, financial planning or business planning require an understanding of the basic concepts of finance. For a small business owner, understanding these concepts will enable him or her to consider how to determine the value of the good, product or service being provided to their customers while also being able to ascertain the cost to operate the business. A corporate executive needs to understand a number of financial concepts including the valuation of a company's stock and the products being provided to consumers as well as the cost of operating the business entity. While this has always been the case for chief executive officers and chief financial officers of publicly traded corporations, it is even more crucial in today's regulatory environment by virtue of the requirements of the Sarbanes-Oxley Act of 2002 (SOX). This Federal regulation requires senior management of publicly traded corporations to attest to the accuracy of the financial statements that these companies are required to file on an annual basis. Not having an understanding of the basic concepts of finance can result in serious consequences for these individuals since there have been felony convictions associated with deficiencies in financial reporting requirements. One can look to the recent history of such companies as Enron and Tyco to realize this.

In the end, small business owners, corporate executives and financial planners are not the only ones who need to understand the basic concepts of finance. In fact, every individual should have some knowledge in this regard since this will enable them to be better equipped to save and invest with confidence, and more importantly avoid acquiring excessive debt. Further, if a person plans on buying a home it can to be helpful to understand how the value of the property is determined, and how much a mortgage to finance the purchase of the dwelling will actually cost. Many people mistakenly believe that owning a home will not cost more than renting an apartment, but this is an incorrect notion at best. There are many costs to consider in addition to the actual payment of the mortgage such as the costs to insure the dwelling, the property taxes, costs of furnishing, payment of utilities and maintenance costs. Not having some basic knowledge regarding finance can result in an individual in not being able to afford the cost of a home. These situations often lead people to acquire excessive consumer debt to cover some of these costs, and paying those debts will hinder their ability to save money — and not saving enough money is the costliest mistake a person can make. By having an understanding of the basic concepts of finance, it is possible to avoid these mistakes and plan for an adequate financial future by saving and investing wisely. At the same time, it is a good idea to consult a professional about financial planning and in that regard, this paper is intended for informational purposes only and should not be considered financial advice.

Terms & Concepts

Asset: Any economic resource owned by a business, institution or individual that has commercial or exchange value.

Asset Valuation: The method for determining the net value of an asset.

Bond: Any debt security that obligates the issuer to pay the bondholder a designated amount of interest at specified intervals and to repay the full amount of the loan at maturity.

Certificate of Deposit: A debt instrument issued by a bank that usually pays interest.

Compound Interest: Interest that was earned on principal plus interest that was earned earlier.

Debt: The generic name for bonds, notes, mortgages and other forms of paper that designate amounts owed and payable on specific dates or on demand.

Defined Benefit Pension Plan: A plan that agrees to pay a pre-determined amount to each person who retires after a certain number of years of service.

Defined Contribution Plan: A pension plan where the contribution amount is set at a specific level while benefits vary depending on the return of investments. In some plans such as a 401(k), 403(b) and a 457, employees make voluntary contributions into a tax deferred account which may or may not be matched by employers.

Financial Planning: The analysis of personal financial circumstances and the design of a program to meet financial needs and objectives.

Government Securities: Securities issued by U.S. government agencies — also called agency securities. Although these securities have high credit ratings, they are not the same as Government Obligations such as Treasury securities and are not backed by the full faith and credit of the U.S. Government.

Investment: The use of capital to generate more money through either income producing outlets or through risk-oriented ventures meant to result in capital gains.

Interest: Cost of using money, conveyed as a rate per specific period of time, usually one year, which is known as an annual rate of interest.

Individual Retirement Account: Also known as an Individual Retirement Arrangement or IRA that is a personal tax-deferred retirement account that an employed person can set up with maximum annual deposits.

Money Market: The market for the issuance purchase and sale of short-term debt instruments.

Money Market Deposit Account: Market sensitive bank account that has a minimum balance requirement ($1,000), limits checks to 3 per month, and the funds for these accounts are considered liquid.

Money Market Fund: Open-ended mutual fund that invests in commercial paper, government securities, certificates of deposit and other highly liquid and safe securities and pays money market rates of interest.

Mutual Fund: Funds owned and operated by investment companies that raises money from shareholders and invests in stocks, bonds, options, or money market securities. The funds offer investors the advantage of diversification and professional money management.

Real Estate: A piece of land and all physical property related to it, including houses, fencing, landscaping, and all rights to the air above and the earth below the property.

Risk Management: The ability to value assets over time in order to minimize the risk of loss of principal.

Savings: An account that pays interest on a day-of-deposit to day-of-withdrawal basis.

Stock: Ownership of a corporation reflected by shares which represent claims against a company's earnings or assets.

Sarbanes-Oxley Act: Federal law requiring senior executives of publicly traded corporations to attest to the accuracy of annual financial statements and that requires internal policies and control procedures to ensure compliance with the act.

Treasury Bill: Negotiable debt instrument of the U.S. Federal Government secured by its full faith and credit and issued at various schedules and maturities.

Bibliography

Brown, M., Haughwout, A., Donghoon, L., & van der Klaauw, W. (2013). The financial crisis at the kitchen table: Trends in household debt and credit. *Current Issues in Economics & Finance, 19*(2), 1-10. Retrieved on November 12, 2013, from EBSCO Online Database Business Source Complete. http://search.ebscohost.com/login.aspx?direct=true&db=bth&AN=88300342&site=ehost-live

Carlson, L. (2005, Oct). Lack of basic financial knowledge impairs retirement. *Employee Benefit News, 19*(13) 18-24. Retrieved on January 18, 2007, from EBSCO Online Database Business Source Premier. http://search.ebscohost.com/login.aspx?direct=true&db=buh&AN=18501264&site=ehost-live

Chatzky, J. Bigda, C. & Jervey, G. (2004, Dec). The six biggest money mistakes and how to avoid them. *Money, 33*(12) 92-101. Retrieved on January 18, 2007, from EBSCO Online Database Business Source Premier. http://search.ebscohost.com/login.aspx?direct=true&db=buh&AN=15060434&site=ehost-live

Clare, M. (2002). Solving the knowledge — value equation (part one). *KM Review, 5*(2) 14-18. Retrieved on January 18, 2007, from EBSCO Online Database Business Source Premier. http://search.ebscohost.com/login.aspx?direct=true&db=buh&AN=6798862&site=ehost-live

Downes, J. & Goodman, J.E. (2006). *Dictionary of financial and investment terms*. Barons Educational Services, Inc. Hauppauge, NY. (Print Content)

Fryar Jr., J., Warther, J., Thibodeau, T., & Drucker, M. (2012). Retirement and estate planning with an emphasis on individual retirement accounts. *Journal of Business*

& *Economics Research, 10*(7), 397-405. Retrieved on November 12, 2013, from EBSCO Online Database Business Source Complete. http://search.ebscohost.com/login.aspx?direct=true&db=bth&AN=80160731&site=ehost-live

Gallo, J.J. (2005). Estate planning conundrums worth repeating. *Journal of Financial Planning, 18*(9) 30-31. Retrieved on January 18, 2007, from EBSCO Online Database Business Source Premier. http://search.ebscohost.com/login.aspx?direct=true&db=buh&AN=17857441&site=ehost-live

Miller, T. (2003). Chapter 2: How to boost your savings. *Kiplinger's Practical Guide to Your Money*, 19-28. Retrieved on January 18, 2007, from EBSCO Online Database Business Source Premier. http://search.ebscohost.com/login.aspx?direct=true&db=buh&AN=9442231&site=ehost-live

Miller, T. (2003). Chapter 3: First, maximize your savings. *Kiplinger's Practical Guide to Your Money*, 31-46. Retrieved on January 18, 2007, from EBSCO Online Database Business Source Premier. http://search.ebscohost.com/login.aspx?direct=true&db=buh&AN=9395859&site=ehost-live

Samavati, H., Adilov, N., & Dilts, D. A. (2013). Empirical analysis of the saving rate in the United States. *Journal of Management Policy & Practice, 14*(2), 46-53. Retrieved on November 12, 2013, from EBSCO Online Database Business Source Complete. http://search.ebscohost.com/login.aspx?direct=true&db=bth&AN=89922139&site=ehost-live

Suggested Reading

Brown, G. & Cliff, M. (2005). Investor sentiment and asset valuation. *Journal of Business, 78*(2) 405-440. Retrieved on January 18, 2007, from EBSCO Online Database Business Source Premier. http://search.ebscohost.com/login.aspx?direct=true&db=buh&AN=17002456&site=ehost-live

Braunstein, S. & Welch, C. (2002, Nov). Financial literacy: An overview of practice, research and policy. *Federal Reserve Bulletin, 88*(11) 445-458. Retrieved on January 18, 2007, from EBSCO Online Database Business Source Premier. http://search.ebscohost.com/login.aspx?direct=true&db=buh&AN=8584843&site=ehost-live

Flaig, J.J. (2005). Improving project selection using expected net present value analysis. *Quality Engineering, 17*(4), 535-538. Retrieved on January 18, 2007, from EBSCO Business Source Premier. http://search.ebscohost.com/login.aspx?direct=true&db=buh&AN=18518221&site=ehost-live

Edited by Richa S. Tiwary, Ph.D., MLS

Dr. Richa S. Tiwary holds a Doctorate in Marketing Management with a specialization in Consumer Behavior from Banaras Hindu University, India. She earned her second Masters in Library Sciences with dual concentration in Information Science & Technology, and, Library Information Services, from the Department of Information Studies, University at Albany-SUNY.

National Elections & Business Cycles

Table of Contents

Abstract

Overview
- Campaign Issues
- Comparing Campaigns & Economic Conditions
- Five Goals of the National Economy
- The Aggregate Demand-Aggregate Supply Model
- Changes in Aggregate Demand
- Fiscal Policy & Monetary Policy

Applications
- National Business Cycles
- Problems in Timing
- Political Business Cycle

Conclusion

Terms & Concepts

Bibliography

Suggested Reading

Abstract

Economic issues receive a great deal of attention during presidential election campaigns in the United States of America as well as in other comparable places around the world. Though a multitude of issues exist, this essay aims to provide a concise framework for drawing contrasts and comparisons between economic issues and events and election campaign statements. One should expect seekers of the presidential office to issue statements about recent job growth, worker productivity, energy supplies, congressional actions, income taxes, and the like. Readers and informed voters can take a step back from those statements or claims and examine them using an aggregate demand-aggregate supply model. It simplifies reality by informing us about the economic state and a primary set of dynamic factors that influence the economy. In addition, one can use the model to contemplate the interdependencies among economic events, fiscal policy, and monetary policy. Armed with an understanding of that framework, readers will gain a better understanding of the cyclical natures of political campaigns and economic events and the critical challenges of synchronizing cycles and policies.

Overview

Economic issues gain prominence during presidential election campaigns in the United States of America and in other places around the globe. Those issues and elections capture the attention of politicians, journalists and scholars from many angles. At the conceptual level, many scholars during the past three decades have focused on the complex relationships between the state of the national economy and the attributes of a presidential office holder or seeker. At the empirical level, it appears that researchers have a lot more work ahead of them in their search to uncover the nature of those relationships. As specific examples of the wide diversity in those efforts, one of the economists referenced in this essay views election results as a function of economic events and another holds the converse view. Acknowledging the uncertainty in the nature of a relationship between a set of presidential election results and a set of economic events, this essay merely serves to inform students and prospective voters by highlighting some key factors and issues that often make their way into presidential and other election campaigns.

Campaign Issues

A range of issues may arise during any given campaign for national office including: Energy prices; environment; health care; antitrust; poverty; crime; education; social security; minimum wage; unions; labor discrimination; international trade; federal spending; income taxes; fiscal policy; national debt; stock markets; monetary policy; interest rates; inflation; and unemployment. Invariably, voters will find the contenders focusing on the last two items in that list. On the one hand, this reduction can simplify matters for voters as they prioritize their own ranking of issues and seek to hear the opposing candidates' views on the issues. On the other hand, some candidates for political office and some students of economics may be familiar with the tradeoff between inflation rates and unemployment rates.

Comparing Campaigns & Economic Conditions

A purpose of this essay is to provide a concise framework for drawing contrasts and comparisons between campaign statements and economic conditions. The median voter model is a tool with which to simplify those economic and political realities. By extension, as already alluded in the paragraph above, candidates for a political office tend to move toward the preferences of the median, or swing, voter. Campaigns seem to increase in complexity and intensity when the results from popular polls indicate that voters are emphasizing one issue over the others. In the pages ahead, readers will find presentations of some economic goals, policies, and variables that tend to surface during political campaigns.

While on the campaign trail, presidential office seekers may make statements about recent job growth, worker productivity, energy supplies, congressional actions, income taxes, and the like. Sometimes the following issues receive little attention or factual data: The status of a federal budget, fiscal policy, and monetary policy; the recent trends in personal income, in income distribution, and in consumer confidence; the rates of unemployment, interest, inflation, and economic growth; and, so on and so forth. Therefore, it is important for politicians, voters, and students to realize some advantages by enhancing their awareness of a critical set of economic measures.

Five Goals of the National Economy

This essay condenses into a few pages a significant portion of information and it points readers toward other sources of information. As a primer available for and conducive to knowledge expansion, for instance, most introductory textbooks in economics list five goals for a national economy. In addition, those books highlight many of the inherent conflicts that exist among and between those goals. As a terse introduction to the conflict between two specific goals, this section begins with a general description of the five goals.

- First in the list is efficiency, which occurs as existing resources generate larger amounts of output in combinations that are valued most by society and consumers.

- Second, full employment occurs when everyone who is eligible for work and desires it actually has a job.

- Third, an equitable distribution of income occurs with the relative movement toward a situation of greater equality in which, for example, ten percent of the population earns ten percent of the income in comparison to a prior situation.

- Fourth, price stability occurs when an inflation rate is as low as possible, stable across time, and consistent with expectations.

- Last, economic growth occurs when there are annual increases in Real Gross Domestic Product (RGDP), which by definition is the constant dollar value of final goods and services produced in the United States during any given year.

To obtain finer detail on these goals, readers again are encouraged to consult textbooks commonly used in introductory undergraduate-level courses in economics including those by Arnold (2005), Guell (2008), and/or McConnell & Brue (2008). Though any contender for the nation's highest political office can refer to any of these goals to launch a debate with their opponent, the rates of economic growth, unemployment, and inflation seem to be the favorite goals in the list. The latter two usually receive the greatest amount of attention and make for a lively and perhaps endless debate. One reason for its presence in a political debate is the inverse relationship between inflation rates and unemployment rates as seen in the Phillips Curve, which is a key concept to keep in mind now and for future reference.

If recent elections are any indication, the trade off will certainly stimulate bantering between opposing candidates and political parties. At this juncture, the reader may begin to imagine how a focus on one side of the equation would add complexity to a public debate between two contenders for a political office. In order to understand that relationship, we need to turn our attention to the basic elements of the national economy.

The Aggregate Demand-Aggregate Supply Model

The aggregate demand-aggregate supply (AD-AS) model informs us about the locus of national output and price level and the set of factors that influence those levels. This section presents the model in a simplified form placing an emphasis on the trade off between inflation and employment. Working in a stepwise manner toward that purpose, readers and students alike become aware of the need to understand graphs and to know that a demand line or curve is downward sloping to the right. This is true whether one is studying microeconomics or macroeconomics. As a specific case in service to this purpose, the supply line or curve in macroeconomics is J-shaped; alternatively, it takes the form of a backward-L shape with a smoothed elbow instead of one with a right angle.

Two key reference points provide essential information. One key reference point is the output level that corresponds with the vertical segment of the AS curve. That segment suggests national output is at its maximum. Another key reference point occurs where the AD and AS curves intersect. That intersection represents the actual macroeconomic equilibrium output and price level. One can then compare an actual output level to a maximum or potential output level in order to interpret the state of the national economy. Keep in mind that those equilibrium points can occur in the horizontal segment or in the vertical segment of the AS or somewhere in between. In other words, the location of the AD is a highly important feature.

General movement of that actual level toward its potential level typically requires a change in aggregate demand and/or a change in aggregate supply. Students also learn that these curves shift rightward or leftward depending upon the stimulus or determinant. In the table below is a summary listing of the determinants of aggregate demand and aggregate supply.

Determinants in the Aggregate Demand-Aggregate Supply Model

Aggregate Demand	Aggregate Supply
Household Expenditures	Worker Productivity
Business Investment Expenditures	Input Prices
Governmental Expenditures & Taxes	Governmental Regulations
Import Expenditures	
Export Expenditures	

In examining a textbook graph with respect to movements in AD and/or AS, one needs to pay particular attention to the horizontal gap between the levels of actual output and maximum or potential output. That attention will allow the reader to ascertain whether the economy needs to expand or contract while recognizing the conflicts among three goals: Economic growth, full employment, and price stability. By extension, one needs to observe changes in the price level that are associated with changes in the actual output levels. By the way, readers should keep in mind that an increase in the price level is, by definition, inflation.

Changes in Aggregate Demand

Let us limit the case to one in which AD changes, which is actually the most dynamic. Furthermore, for the sake of brevity, the critical focuses are governmental expenditures and business investment expenditures. For reasons presented in more detail in the next section, any increase in these two forms of expenditures is likely to move AD rightward possibly inducing increases in the level of real output and/or possibly generating increases in the price level. When AD continues to move rightward in the horizontal segment of the AS, for instance, the actual output level rises without inflation. This means that the economy is expanding and growing; adding more workers into the production process, and increasing personal incomes.

Should the rightward movement of the AD enter into the intermediate range or elbow segment of the AS, then outputs, employments, and incomes continue to increase but so does the price level. It is in this intermediate range where the trade off between inflation and employment is most visible. As AD continues to shift rightward, equilibrium will eventually occur in the vertical segment of the AS. This means that output becomes static and inflation rates become larger. In order to reduce inflationary pressures, something needs to prompt a leftward shift in AD thereby inducing decreases in outputs, employments, and incomes.

Those decreases can result from reductions in investment expenditures and/or in government expenditures. Changes in government expenditures can occur directly through fiscal policy. Changes in investment expenditures can occur indirectly through monetary policy and its effect on interest rates. It is important to remember that investment is typically a direct function of interest rates. This means that an increase (a decrease) in interest rates prompts a decrease (an increase) in business investment expenditures. As critical components that influence economic events and activity levels, monetary policy and fiscal policy are the subjects of the next section.

Fiscal Policy & Monetary Policy

These two types of policy influence the state of a national economy. Fiscal policy refers to the use of federal tax revenues and governmental expenditures for purposes of managing national output, employment, and income levels.

- Fiscal policy usually results in an increase or a decrease in aggregate demand though changes in business taxes can increase or decrease aggregate supply. Because it takes a lot of time and negotiation to get a tax or spending plan through Congress and final endorsement by the President, monetary policy is relatively faster and more flexible than fiscal policy.

- Monetary policy is the other policy tool by which banking officials actively manage the level of economic activity at the national level. In contrast to fiscal policy, it involves actions by the Federal Reserve System, in conjunction with the United States Treasury, for purposes such as changing the nation's supply of money in order to increase or decrease key interest rates. Furthermore, the results of monetary policy influence the level of aggregate demand by providing various financial incentives for households and/or businesses to alter their spending plans through increases or decreases in their expenditures.

Some textbooks refer to monetary policy as the artful management of price level, business cycle smoothing, employment levels, and economic growth rates. To be the most effective, both monetary policy and fiscal policy require accurate timing and a precise estimation of economic state. In the next section, we turn our attention to applications of those policies and the aforementioned concepts and abstract relationships to real events beginning with coverage of business cycles.

Applications

Armed with an understanding of the conceptual framework as represented by the AD-AS model and its relationship to fiscal and monetary policies, readers are now ready to consider applying those components to the cyclical natures of political campaigns and economic events. In general, this section will present the reader with coverage of business and political cycles and some integral problems with respect to the timing of actions. More specifically, the reader will gain a better understanding of the difficulties in associating national economic performance with individual or group efforts to manipulate the economy.

National Business Cycles

Real gross domestic product (RGDP) oscillates naturally in wave-like form over time and through four phases of what we call the business cycle. Let's progress through the cycle starting with an upturn or increase in RGDP, which defines the expansionary phase as it continues upward until reaching the peak phase. Moving past the peak is the downturn or decrease in RGDP, which defines the contractionary phase as it continues downward until reaching the trough phase.

A section of the contractionary phase may contain an economic recession, which by official definition is a decrease in RGDP that occurs for six or more consecutive months. Economic growth, which by definition is an increase in RGDP throughout time, is sometimes observable over several business cycles. In other words, a comparison of the cycle peak-to-peak will reveal economic growth when there is an upward trend across those peaks. Consider the addition of some numbers to the business cycle.

The duration of the business cycle varies and is measurable in months. According to the National Bureau of Economic Research and data from the past 50 years or so, an economic contraction lasts about 17 months on average and an economic expansion lasts about 38 months. Certainly, most individuals would prefer to minimize the length of time in a contraction and to maximize it in the expansion. Examining that data with optimism, the average economic contraction lasts about 10 months and the expansion lasts about 57 months. Consequently, it seems highly likely that any presidential term in office will encounter a favorable and/or an unfavorable oscillation in the business cycle. A longstanding and unresolved issue is whether a relationship exists between economic events and office holders.

One long stream of research concerning the influences of economic events and incumbency characteristics on election outcomes is available through the works of Fair (1996). Those studies provide some evidence that economic growth rates and inflation rates are reliable and valid predictors of election outcomes. In brief, the work by Fair also suggests that voters tend to compare parties on the basis of economic events that occurred both recently and during the entire term in office. Most importantly, those works illuminate how the relative currency of economic events relates to election results while providing additional insight with respect to the complex role of timing.

Problems in Timing

In terms of the challenges that timing presents, this section of the essay shifts the attention of readers from the influence of timing on elections to its influence on national policy formation and implementation. Certainly, it takes time for decision makers and policies to work toward accomplishing the five economic goals. Furthermore, the decision processes often begin with an attempt to pinpoint which of the five goals need attention and when.

Textbooks in economics usually point to three lags or types of problems with regard to timing.

- First, the recognition lag advances the idea that it takes time to measure state of economy. For example, although data collections are ongoing, the tabulation and analysis of that data take time before a larger picture emerges.

- Second, the administrative lag advances the notion that it takes time to craft an agreement on a specific course of action. For example, it literally takes an act of Congress, which is very time consuming, when formulating fiscal policy.

- The third is the operational lag, which advances the view that it takes time to realize an impact from the policy initiative.

Analysts can ultimately assess the effectiveness of the monetary policy or the fiscal policy of choice, but long after the problem identification and resolution phases are complete. Usually hindsight clarifies vision, which may or may not translate into foresight. Additional complications may enter the next round of policy formation especially when political elections draw near.

Political Business Cycle

Timing is critical when attempting to smooth the business cycle. It is also a highly challenging component for those who seriously contemplate an appropriate course of action with respect to monetary policy and/or fiscal policy. At this juncture, reader attention shifts from efforts considering the five economic goals to those considering one goal-election or re-election. According to an unfavorable and perhaps realistic perspective on those actions, some candidates for political office will pursue election campaign strategies to attract the attention of the median voter and others. In doing so, they are partaking in and perpetuating the political business cycle.

These actions amount to politically-motivated fiscal policy, which aims for short-term improvement in the economic state just before national elections (Guell, 2008). Drawing from the information presented earlier regarding business cycles and so on, pre-election tax cuts or spending increases may be entirely inappropriate for the current state of the national economy. Some economists suggest that expansionary fiscal policy usually occurs before elections and contractionary fiscal policy usually occurs afterwards though they assert that the evidence is virtually nonexistent or weak, suggesting the genuine need for further inquiry. Furthermore, one may wonder whether politicians look to monetary policy in case fiscal policy is temporarily unavailable due to budgetary stalemates between those politicians on Capitol Hill and those in the White House. At any rate, some economists assert that monetary policy is more expedient, flexible, and politically palatable though it is typically considered a longer reach for politicians in comparison to fiscal policy.

Those policies, whether taken separately or together, represent the capacity to affect the state of the national economy. In terms of the interrelationship between presidential terms and economic growth rates, Table 11.1 in Guell (2008; p. 150) provides some relevant data and descriptive statistics suggesting that growth rates in the fourth year of a term, on average, are slightly higher than those for the first year of a term. Those data are available from the Bureau of Economic Analysis, which is a subunit of the US Department of Commerce.

At the least, the tabulations from Guell (2008) and the findings from Fair (1996) emphasize the need for additional work clarifying the nature of interrelationships among economic events, national elections, and the behaviors of politicians and voters. In summary, this essay aims to temper the notion of causation between a presidential figure and the national economic state. Furthermore, the author hopes that readers and informed voters alike are more prepared, in part because of this essay, to recognize questionable statements about economic events whether they originate from presidential candidates, elected officials, and/or journalists.

Conclusion

In closing, this essay represents an attempt to help readers primarily understand some key economic concepts and variables and secondarily for them to build the capacity to see more clearly through the usual hyperbole surrounding election campaigns.

Terms & Concepts

Administrative Lag: A problem in timing attributable to the amount of time required to craft an agreement for addressing the economic state.

Aggregate Demand: The amount of real domestic output that households, businesses, governments, and foreign buyers collectively desire at given price levels.

Aggregate Supply: The amount of real domestic output available at given price levels.

Business Cycle: Regular patterns of upswings and downturns in Real Gross Domestic Product over time through the following four phases: Expansion, peak, contraction, and trough.

Economic Contraction: A decrease in Real Gross Domestic Product over time.

Economic Expansion: An increase in Real Gross Domestic Product over time.

Economic Growth: An upward trend in Real Gross Domestic Product over several business cycles.

Efficiency: The outcome from producing more output with the same or lesser amounts of input.

Equitable Distribution of Income: Observed as the distribution of income becomes more equal; for example, arrival at the point at which 10 percent of the population earns 10 percent of the national income from a point of inequality.

Fiscal Policy: Actions by Congress and the President to alter the economic state involving changes in government expenditures and in tax rates.

Inflation: A general rise in the overall level of prices; measured using the Gross Domestic Product deflator and/or the Consumer Price Index.

Full Employment: Occurs when the unemployment rate is at its lowest point, without inflation.

Monetary Policy: Actions by the Federal Reserve System to alter the economic state involving changes in interest rates.

Operational Lag: A problem in timing attributable to the amount of time required for assessing the impact of policies on the economic state.

Political Business Cycle: Occurs with an engagement of fiscal policy for short-term gain for the explicit purpose of obtaining votes during political election campaigns.

Price Stability: The state in which the price level is constant and/or the inflation rate remains unchanged.

Real Gross Domestic Product: An inflation-adjusted measure for the dollar value of all final goods and services produced domestically during the course of one fiscal year.

Recognition Lag: A problem in timing attributable to the amount of time required for obtaining measurements on the economic state.

Bibliography

Aguiar-Conraria, L., Magalhães, P., & Soares, M. (2013). The nationalization of electoral cycles in the United States: a wavelet analysis. *Public Choice, 156*(3/4), 387-408. Retrieved November 15, 2013, from EBSCO Online Database Business Source Complete. http://search.ebscohost.com/login.aspx?direct=true&db=bth&AN=89047054&site=ehost-live

Arnold, R.A. (2005). *Economics*(7th ed.) Mason, OH: Thomson South-Western.

Canes-Wrone, B., & Park, J. (2012). Electoral business cycles in OECD countries. *American Political Science Review, 106*(1), 103-122.Retrieved November 15, 2013, from EBSCO Online Database Business Source Complete. http://search.ebscohost.com/login.aspx?direct=true&db=bth&AN=72675591&site=ehost-live

Fair, R. (1996). Econometrics and presidential elections. *Journal of Economic Perspectives, 10*(3), 89-102. Retrieved December 20, 2007, from EBSCO Online Database Business Source Premier. http://search.ebscohost.com/login.aspx?direct=true&db=buh&AN=9610023620&site=ehost-live

Guell, R. C. (2008). *Issues in economics today*(4th ed.). Boston, MA: McGraw-Hill Irwin.

Julio, B., & Yook, Y. (2012). Political uncertainty and corporate investment cycles. *Journal of Finance, 67*(1), 45-84. Retrieved November 15, 2013, from EBSCO Online Database Business Source Complete. http://search.ebscohost.com/login.aspx?direct=true&db=bth&AN=70359944&site=ehost-live

McConnell, C. R. & Brue, S. L. (2008). *Economics*(17th ed.). Boston, MA: McGraw-Hill Irwin.

Suggested Reading

Alesina, A., Rubini, N. & Cohen, G. (1997). *Political cycles and the macroeconomy.* Cambridge, MA: MIT Press.

Blomberg, S., & Hess, G. (2003). Is the political business cycle for real? *Journal of Public Economics, 87*(5/6), 1091. Retrieved December 20, 2007, from EBSCO Online Datbase Business Source Premier. http://search.ebscohost.com/login.aspx?direct=true&db=buh&AN=9656581&site=ehost-live

Boix, C. (1997). Political parties and the supply side of the economy: The provision of physical and human capital. *American Journal of Political Science, 41*(3), 814. Retrieved December 20, 2007, from EBSCO Online Database Business Source Premier. http://search.ebscohost.com/login.aspx?direct=true&db=buh&AN=9707154096&site=ehost-live

Drazen, A. (2000). The political business cycle after 25 years. *NBER/Macroeconomics Annual, 15*(1), 75-117. Retrieved December 20, 2007, from EBSCO Online Database Business Source Premier. http://search.ebscohost.com/login.aspx?direct=true&db=buh&AN=5123135&site=ehost-live

Klein, M. (1996). Timing is all: Elections and the duration of United States business cycles. *Journal of Money, Credit & Banking, 28*(1), 84-101. Retrieved December 20, 2007, from EBSCO Online Database Business Source Premier. http://search.ebscohost.com/login.aspx?direct=true&db=buh&AN=9603271066&site=ehost-live

Essay by Steven R. Hoagland, Ph.D.

Dr. Hoagland holds a baccalaureate and a master degree in economics, a master of urban studies, and a doctorate in urban services management with a cognate in education. His professional background includes service as senior-level university administrator responsible for planning, assessment, and research. It also includes winning multi-million dollar grants, both as a sponsored programs administrator and as a proposal development team member with expertise in research design and program evaluation consultant. In addition to his service to the health care, the information technology, and the education sectors, he facilitates learning as an adjunct professor of economics and has taught more than 50 courses as a part-time faculty member. When time and resources permit, as the founding executive director of a nonprofit organization launched in 2007, he guides college-bound high school students toward a more objective and simplified method of college selection, which holds promise for improve the return on their investments in higher learning.

Capital Budgeting

Table of Contents

Abstract

Overview

Further Insights

    Capital Budgeting Valuation Methods

    Net Present Value (NPV)

    Internal Rate of Return (IRR)

    Discounted Cash Flow (DCF)

    Payback Period

Issues

    Economic Issues in Capital Budgeting Decisions

    A Capital Budgeting Issue for U.S. Steel Producers

    The Capital Budgeting Decisions of Small Companies

    Investment Activity

    Planning Activity

    Project Evaluation Technique

    Analysis Conclusions

    The Results of an Analysis of Budgeting Strategies of U.S. Multinational Subsidiaries

Conclusion

Terms & Concepts

Bibliography

Suggested Reading

Abstract

Capital budgeting is the process of determining whether or not a company should invest in projects such as new facilities or products. This article presents the most common methods of capital budgeting; discusses economic issues in capital budgeting unique to three types of companies: Steel producers, small companies, and U.S. multinational subsidiaries; and provides a glossary of relevant terms.

Overview

When a company plans to invest in new facilities, equipment, or products, it may engage in capital budgeting. Capital budgeting is a strategy that a company can utilize to plan future investment projects.

A company utilizes capital budgeting to establish whether a project's benefits will outweigh the costs of investing in the project. The process generally involves constructing a formula that considers total funds needed for the project, including working capital; the financial benefits expected from the project; the length of time needed to reap the financial benefits of the project; and whether it is better to forego the project completely. For example, a company that manufactures furniture is considering whether or not to also start manufacturing its own fabric for the furniture. The furniture manufacturer can use capital budgeting to determine the most financially profitable option for manufacturing fabric among the following four investment projects:

- Remodel a current facility to accommodate a fabric manufacturing operation.
- Build a new fabric manufacturing facility.
- Purchase an existing fabric manufacturing company.
- Continue to purchase the fabric rather than manufacture it. (If this option is chosen, the project is then removed from consideration as a capital budgeting project.)

Further Insights

As part of the capital budgeting process, companies consider their access to funds; their need for cash flow to operate the company throughout the timeline for any capital budgeting project; and in some instances, their responsibility to shareholders.

Capital Budgeting Valuation Methods

A variety of approaches and mathematical formulas may be used in capital budgeting. Four of the most common approaches used in capital budgeting are based on the following four valuation methods:

- Net Present Value (NPV)
- Internal Rate of Return (IRR)
- Discounted Cash Flow (DCF)
- Payback Period

Net Present Value (NPV)

The first capital budgeting valuation method is net present value (NPV). NPV reflects the variance between the current amount of cash inflows and the current amount of cash outflows. Present value refers to the current worth of money that will be received in the future, based on a particular rate of return.

Internal Rate of Return (IRR)

The second capital budgeting valuation method is internal rate of return (IRR). IRR, which is sometimes called economic rate of return, refers to the discount rate that renders the NPV of all cash flows for a specific project equal to zero. Usually, the higher the IRR for a specific project, the more financially attractive the project will be.

Discounted Cash Flow (DCF)

The third capital budgeting valuation method is discounted cash flow (DCF). In DCF, future free cash flows are discounted to arrive at a present value. For a project to be considered worthwhile according to this valuation method, the DCF must be greater than the present investment cost.

Payback Period

The last capital budgeting valuation method is payback period. The payback period refers to the amount of time needed to recapture the cost of an investment. In general, the sooner a company can recover the cost of their investment, the more financially attractive the project will be.

The payback method of valuation does not measure the time value of money or reflect any financial benefits that would occur after the payback period. Therefore, this method of capital budgeting is considered less effective than the NPV, IRR, or DCF methods.

Issues

Economic Issues in Capital Budgeting Decisions

In addition to considering their corporate financial goals, companies need to also consider how national and international economic issues will affect their capital budgeting decisions.

This section explores three topics that consider the economic issues that affect capital budgeting:

- A capital budgeting issue for U.S. steel producers.
- The capital budgeting decisions of small companies.
- The results of an analysis of capital budgeting strategies of U.S. multinational subsidiaries.

A Capital Budgeting Issue for U.S. Steel Producers

The first economic issue in capital budgeting covers a capital budgeting issue for U.S. steel producers.

Should U.S. steel producers expand their capacity in order to avoid being the lowest-cost suppliers to the U.S. market? At least one industry analyst says "No." Michelle Applebaum, an independent steel industry analyst, discusses why she disagrees with those who think that U.S. steel producers need to expand their capacity (production) in order to prosper in the marketplace.

Applebaum offers three reasons why expanding capacity isn't desirable:

- Limited resources, such as scrap metal, are available.
- The delivery of steelmaking equipment requires an exceptionally long lead time.
- The potential for a surge in exports from China remains an economic threat.

She reasons that any capital budgeting that includes a new capacity project would have to assume a period of negative returns in order to yield a net positive return (Applebaum, 2007, p. 91).

Instead of investing in capital budgeting projects to increase production capacity, Applebaum suggest that it would be more mutually beneficial for steel producers and their customers to engage in the following practices:

- **Steel producers:** Allow for flexible arrangements with customers. Reduce volume when business conditions warrant this practice, rather than forcing customers to buy according to previous contract arrangements.
- **Customers:** Honor your price commitments with the producers.

- **Steel Producers and Customers:** Share surcharge responsibility. Surcharges allow visibility into pricing for raw materials and as such are necessary, but producers can show flexibility; when the prices of raw materials decrease they can decrease the surcharges.

The Capital Budgeting Decisions of Small Companies

The second economic issue in capital budgeting covers the capital budgeting decisions of small companies.

Based on data compiled by the National Federation of Independent Business, Danielson and Scott (2006) analyzed the capital budgeting decisions of small businesses. Although the U.S. Small Business Administration defines small businesses as those with lesss than 500 employees, Danielson and Scott based their study on companies with fewer than 250 employees.

Danielson and Scott based their study on 792 observations and segmented the industries into four groups: Service; construction and manufacturing; retail/wholesale; and other. Their analysis of the data addressed three aspects of capital budgeting in small companies:

- Investment Activity
- Planning Activity
- Project Evaluation Technique

Investment Activity

The first aspect of capital budgeting in small companies that is addressed is investment activity. For companies in the construction and manufacturing industries, their most significant investments during the previous year were almost evenly distributed among replacement of equipment, expansion of existing products, and introduction of a new product line.

Planning Activity

The second aspect of capital budgeting in small companies that is addressed is planning activity. For companies in the construction and manufacturing industries, 68% made cash flow projections before making a major investment; 32% wrote a business plan; and 71% considered their tax situation.

Project Evaluation Technique

The last aspect of capital budgeting in small companies that is addressed is project evaluation technique. The majority of construction and manufacturing companies (22%) used an informal "gut feel" method to determine whether a project was financially attractive. At 19%, the payback period method was the second most popular evaluation technique in capital budgeting among this group of companies.

Analysis Conclusions

In summary, Danielson and Scott (2006) concluded that the capital budgeting strategies of small companies are often characterized by the following factors:

- They frequently balanced wealth maximization against objectives such as maintaining the independence of the business.
- They often lacked the personnel and resources to complete in-depth capital budgeting analyses.
- They frequently relied upon either the payback period method of capital budgeting or the owner's "gut feeling." This practice contrasts with that of large companies, who were more likely to use the discounted cash flow analysis method.

The Results of an Analysis of Budgeting Strategies of U.S. Multinational Subsidiaries

The last economic issue in capital budgeting covers the budgeting strategies of U.S. multinational subsidiaries.

According to a study by Hasan, Shao, & Shao (1997) of 159 foreign subsidiaries of U.S.-based multinational manufacturing enterprises operating in 43 companies, additional influences complicate the capital budgeting decisions of multinational subsidiaries. They identified the following five complicating factors(Hasan, Shao, & Shao, 1997, p. 68):

- Complex Cash Flow Estimates;
- Foreign Exchange Rate Fluctuations;
- Varying Accounting Systems;
- Financial Risks;
- Political Uncertainties.

The authors determined that the capital budgeting process for multinational enterprises is affected by factors that do not affect domestic companies.

Based on their analysis of the survey respondents' responses, they reached the following conclusions (Hasan et al., 1997, p. 75):

- The refinement of the capital budgeting strategies of foreign subsidiaries correlated to levels of ownership status and financial leverage. In general, in those situations where the parent companies owned most of the subsidiaries' shares, more sophisticated capital budgeting strategies were likely to be employed.

- The sources used to determine discount rates were positively related to the age of the firm, total asset size, and whether the subsidiaries were publicly traded.

- Publicly traded subsidiaries, firms with credit regulations implemented by outside creditors, and asset size were closely associated with refined risk-adjustment capital budgeting strategies.

Conclusion

When a company engages in capital budgeting, it carefully assesses which projects are most important to the company's strategy and financial future because capital budgeting projects will consume a large financial investment and greatly affect operating cash flow. Capital budgeting projects therefore must take into account whether the future benefits of the projects will outweigh the financial investment and whether the company can afford to financially support the project and also continue operating the company for the duration of the capital projects.

Various methods and mathematical formulas are available for capital budgeting. Most large companies will choose one of the three most popular capital budgeting methods: Net present value (NPV), internal rate of return (IRR), or discounted cash flow (DCF). Small companies with fewer than 250 employees, choose the "gut feeling" approach to capital budgeting most frequently, followed by the payback period method. The payback period method is more attractive to smaller companies because it relies upon the shortest possible time to recapture the cost of the investment in the project. However, the payback period method does not measure profitability because it does not take into account any benefits that accrue after the payback period and it also does not account for the time value of money. For these reasons, the payback method of capital budgeting is not used as frequently by larger companies, who are usually in a better position to wait longer to recoup their investments. The capital budgeting strategies for the foreign subsidiaries of U.S multinational companies are complicated by five unique factors: Complex cash flow estimates; foreign exchange rate fluctuations; varying accounting systems; financial risks; and political uncertainties.

Terms & Concepts

Capital Budgeting: The strategy used by businesses to plan out the viability of future investments.

Cash Flow: The cash flow statement demonstrates the amount of cash produced and spent by a company during a certain time period, measured by adding non-cash charges (including depreciation) to net income post-taxes. Cash flow can be associated with a certain project or to a whole company. Cash flow can be used to represent a company's financial viability.

Cash Inflows: Mainly generated from one of three activities: financing, operations, or investing. Cash inflows can also occur through donations or gifts.

Cash Outflows: Result from expenses or investments.

Discounted Cash Flow (DCF): A valuation strategy utilized to determine the benefits of an investment opportunity. DCF analysis looks at future free cash flow predictions and discounts them (usually using the weighted average capital cost) to reach a present value, which is then used to assess the investment possibility. If the value derived from DCF is greater than the present investment cost, the opportunity might be an attractive one.

Free Cash Flow: A measurement of financial strength measured by subtracting capital expenditures from operating cash flow. Free cash flow demonstrates the cash that a company can produce without including the funds necessary to upkeep or add to its base assets.

Internal Rate of Return (IRR), also known as Economic Rate of Return (ERR): The discount rate employed during capital budgeting analysis that equates the net current value of all cash flows from a given project to zero. Usually a higher internal rate of return means that a project is a more attractive proposition. Companies can use this rating to evaluate a number of potential projects. With all other factors staying consistent between projects, the project with the highest IRR would most likely be chosen.

Manufacture: To make a product from raw materials by hand or by machine.

Net Present Value (NPV): The variation between the current amount of cash inflow and the current amount of cash outflow. NPV is used during capital budgeting to assess the profitability of a potential investment or future project.

Payback Period: The amount of time necessary to recapture an investment cost. If all other factors are consistent, the best investment is the one with the shortest payback period.

Present Value (PV), also known as Discounted Value: The present value of a future sum of money or cash flows given a certain return rate. Future cash flows are discounted at the discount rate. The higher the discount rate is, then the lower the current value of the future cash flows will be. Identifying the accurate discount rate is critical to effectively determining the value of future cash flows, regardless of whether they are earnings or obligations. The basic premise is that receiving $1,000 at the present is more valuable than receiving the same $1,000 in five years because during the intervening five years you could have invested it and received addition returns.

Small Businesses: Danielson & Scott (2006) cite the U.S. Small Business Administration definition of small businesses as "firms with fewer than 500 employees." However, the U.S. Small Business Administration actually limits the size based on industry according to the North American Industry Classification System (NAICS).

Bibliography

Applebaum, M. (2007). Three reasons why upping US capacity doesn't add up. *American Metal Market, 116*(6), 91-91.

Retrieved November 29, 2007, from EBSCO Online Database Business Source Complete. http://search.ebscohost.com/login.aspx?direct=true&db=bth&AN=27571662&site=ehost-live

Bower, J.L, & Gilbert, C.G. (2007). How managers' everyday decisions create or destroy your company's strategy. *Harvard Business Review, 85*(2), 72-79. Retrieved November 26, 2007, from EBSCO Online Database Business Source Complete. http://search.ebscohost.com/login.aspx?direct=true&db=bth&AN=23691173&site=ehost-live

Danielson, M.G., & Scott, J.A. (2006). Capital budgeting decisions of small businesses. *Journal of Applied Finance, 16*(2), 45 56. Retrieved November 26, 2007, from EBSCO Online Database Business Source Complete. http://search.ebscohost.com/login.aspx?direct=true&db=bth&AN=25301697&site=ehost-live

GERVAIS, S., HEATON, J. B., & ODEAN, T. (2011). Overconfidence, Compensation Contracts, and Capital Budgeting. *Journal Of Finance*, 66(5), 1735-1777. Retrieved November 24, 2013, from EBSCO Online Database Business Source Complete. http://search.ebscohost.com/login.aspx?direct=true&db=bth&AN=65577980&site=ehost-live

Ghahremani, M., Aghaie, A., & Abedzadeh, M. (2012). Capital Budgeting Technique Selection through Four Decades: With a Great Focus on Real Option *International Journal Of Business & Management*, 7(17), 98-119 Retrieved November 24, 2013, from EBSCO Online Database Business Source Complete. http://search.ebscohost.com/login.aspx?direct=true&db=bth&AN=80037203&site=ehost-live

Hasan, I., Shao, L.P., & Shao, A.T. (1997). Determinants of capital budgeting strategies: An econometric analysis of U.S. multinational subsidiaries. *Multinational Business Review, 5*(1), 68-76. Retrieved November 26, 2007, from EBSCO Online Database Business Source Complete. http://search.ebscohost.com/login.aspx?direct=true&db=bth&AN=9702182150&site=ehost-live

Investopedia. (2007). *Dictionary*. Retrieved November 26, 2007, from http://www.investopedia.com/dictionary/default.asp

Merriam-Webster's collegiate dictionary (10th ed.). (2000). Springfield, MA: Merriam- Webster.

U.S. Small Business Administration. Web site. Retrieved December 4, 2007, from http://www.sba.gov/services/contractingopportunities/sizestandardstopics/size/index.html

Wolffsen, P. (2012). Modification of capital budgeting under uncertainty. *Applied Economics: Systematic Research*, 6(2), 143-159. Retrieved November 24, 2013, from EBSCO Online Database Business Source Complete. http://search.ebscohost.com/login.aspx?direct=true&db=bth&AN=84518419&site=ehost-live

Suggested Reading

Bimal, N., et al. (2007). A quality-based business model for determining non-product investment: A case study from a Ford automotive engine plant. *Engineering Management Journal, 19*(3), 41-56. Retrieved November 26, 2007, from EBSCO Online Database Business Source Complete. http://search.ebscohost.com/login.aspx?direct=true&db=bth&AN=27350377&site=ehost-live

Dedi, L., & Orsag, S. (2007). Capital budgeting practices: A survey of Croatian firms. *South East European Journal of Economics & Business, 2*(1), 59-67. Retrieved November 26, 2007, from EBSCO Online Database Business Source Complete. http://search.ebscohost.com/login.aspx?direct=true&db=bth&AN=25657478&site=ehost-live

Hyde, J., Dunn, J.W., Steward, A., & Hollabaugh, E.R. (2007). Robots don't get sick or get paid overtime, but are they a profitable option for milking cows? *Review of Agricultural Economics, 29*(2), 366-380. Retrieved November 26, 2007, from EBSCO Online Database Business Source Complete. http://search.ebscohost.com/login.aspx?direct=true&db=bth&AN=24594303&site=ehost-live

Essay by Sue Ann Connaughton, MLS

Sue Ann Connaughton is a freelance writer and researcher. Formerly, she was the Manager of Intellectual Capital & Research at Silver Oak Solutions, a spend management solutions consulting firm that was acquired by CGI in 2005. Ms. Connaughton holds a Bachelor of Arts in English from Salem State College, a Master of Education from Boston University, and a Master of Library & Information Science from Florida State University.

Financial Management in Business

Table of Contents

Abstract

Overview

Applications

    Operational Financial Management

    Critical Reports & Tools for Financial Managers

    Operational Challenges

    Case Study: Department of Homeland Security & Oversight

    Recommendations for Department of Homeland Security

    Discourse

    Public vs. Private Oversight

    Sarbanes Oxley Law

    The Raytheon Fraud Initiative

Conclusion

Terms & Concepts

Bibliography

Suggested Reading

Abstract

This essay delivers an overview of the role of the financial manager, in both the private and the public sector. Non-profit organizations are not specifically included in this discussion. A brief review of some standard mechanisms business managers use to monitor financial performance is followed by a larger discussion of the evolving role of financial and business managers, including cautionary notes to those new to the role. Emphasis is placed on internal oversight and monitoring mechanisms; integral parts of effective business accounting which support the plans, methods, and procedures used to meet the company's goals and objectives. It will become readily apparent to the reader that financial reporting, using the traditional tools described herein, is clearly evolving into a more complex and integrated process, not unlike the globalization occurring in many industries. Integration of business processes in lockstep with financial administration is critical to maintain a competitive position in the marketplace. This article highlights the transformations in accountancy and internal practice seen in the marketplace today, and how these changes are bringing about an evolution of the role for those in key positions related to financial management.

Overview

Business leadership is responsible for communicating the organization's expectations, measures, and goals to those responsible for implementing the action plans set forth to meet the organization's objectives. Financial managers establish and monitor performance measures, sometimes termed "scorecards," in today's business environment. There exists an old adage that anything not measured cannot be improved; it is paramount that measures are tracked and charted as part of routine reporting. Financial metrics are increasingly transparent to stakeholders as they offer a robust means to monitor fiscal accountability. The role of the financial manager in the eighties and nineties brings to mind a picture of the bespectacled accountant, donning a green banker's visor, and poring over books under a glowing lamp in the evening office. The 21st century financial manager wears many hats and answers to multiple stakeholders who require manifold levels of accountability. Systems, people and technology impact the financial performance of complex organizations, and it is no surprise that managers find themselves in an evolving milieu which challenges historical paradigms.

The definition of financial management, in broad terms, describes financial performance oversight practiced by individuals, business entities and public domains. More specifically, financial controls, assessed routinely by decision-makers, provide oversight of the entity's financial structure and function. Supervising short-term activities and long-term strategies while protecting stakeholders' interests, falls under the authority of the manager's leadership. Augmenting front-line oversight, publicly-owned businesses undergo independent accounting audits of their financial statements with comment by the auditor, aimed at providing an objective review of the business' fiscal status. Oversight in the public sector has become more highly regulated, but even in the non-public sector, financial managers are facing substantial change, with intense scrutiny and accountability for performance becoming the norm. As performance indicators are more intensely examined, knowledge of historical and future trends must be a priority for those in financial leadership roles. Managers' liability for actions of those and of others in their area of control is today's new reality.

Michael Goldstein, of CPA Journal reports "191 out of 250 executives responded to questions on business finance management at the AICPA Benchmarking and Financial Engineering Conference in New Orleans. The survey, conducted by the AICPA's Management Accounting Executive Committee, laid the groundwork for the Institute's "Financial Management" 2000 {conference}. Nearly 81% of U.S. senior financial executives expected to see more sweeping changes in the core financial functions at their companies, while approximately 58% already had seen such changes, according to a survey by the AICPA. The respondents, 98% of whom described themselves as financial controllers and above at their companies, cited transaction processing, performance measurement, management reporting, and budgeting as among the examples of basic functions that most needed reengineering" (Goldstein, 1995).

Applications

Operational Financial Management

A company's fiscal reports provide the data upon which the manager performs his or her financial analysis; reporting should provide key information about the business' prior, current and projected performance. Analysis must be timely to be effective; managers are responsible for ensuring accuracy and applicability of the data while striving to achieve information systems capable of capturing and reporting useful data to support this work. "'In today's swiftly changing business environment, U.S. companies will have to learn to tap into powerful information technology to ensure proper financial controls without continuing to waste critical resources on unnecessary layers of transaction processing,' said Dr. John K. Shank, chairman of the AICPA's Management Accounting Executive Committee and professor of managerial accounting at the Amos Tuck School of Business at Dartmouth College" (Goldstein, 1995). Fortunately with advances in technology, timeliness and accessibility of financial information, decision-making is dramatically better than it has ever been.

Critical Reports & Tools for Financial Managers

For managers coming out of business schools, the following list offers an inventory of critical reports and tools long-heralded by business as key needs for every financial manager. The list is by no means inclusive of all financial reporting mechanisms utilized in today's business world.

- **Income Statements,** by their very nature, provide utility when timely and accurate. Generally Accepted Accounting Principles (GAAP) direct that the income statement follow a relatively standard format that starts with revenue and subtracts from revenue the costs of running the business. Net income, also known as net profit (or net loss) represents the "bottom line" for an entity over a set accounting period. The income statement may be enhanced to include budgeted revenues and expenses with variance percentages; highlights for initial screening of concerns for the busy manager. Variances, particularly those that are material (threshold varies), are a base upon which the financial manager forms her analysis and next steps.

- The Cash Flow Statement (CFS) is the financial statement, generated at routine intervals, that shows a company's incoming and outgoing cash funds: Where the money is coming from and where it is being used. The statement reports the cash flow in terms of investment, operating and financing activities. The CFS is used to evaluate the short-term viability of a company, most particularly its ability to pay its operating bills, including payroll and other immediate expenses. Banks, lenders and creditors also rely on this information to assess the company's ability to repay loans. In today's highly competitive resources environment, businesses must realize that potential employees' comfort with the viability of the company is as critically important as the opinion of the interested parties mentioned earlier.

- The Balance Sheet is commonly referred to as the "snapshot" of the business' assets and liabilities at a finite point in time. Essentially, the document provides balances of assets which equal liabilities and net worth. The balance sheet is the one document which reports to a single point in time, rather than a period of time, such as the Profit and Loss statement.

- **Accounts Receivable** is managed in large companies through credit control, collections and payment processing; safeguarding assets means tracking the average number of days it takes to collect an account (Salek, 2007). The accounts receivable is mentioned in this article because of its direct impact on cash flow, the necessity of which was addressed in the prior paragraph. Astute managers are on the alert for lengthening collection periods, a heralding sign of potentially decreasing cash flow. Availing customers of the benefit of purchasing goods and services on credit can build a larger customer base; but savvy financial experts know this practice does need to be managed aggressively in order to stay financially protected. In times of sales or economic slowdown, too high an AR can disadvantage the company greatly. The percentage of receivables over 90 days is monitored by managers to gain high-level views of how the sales and collections staff is performing. The older a receivable account grows, the more risk to the creditor (the business) and the less value to the collected dollar. Managers simply cannot lose sight of this important marker which keeps them abreast of concerning areas of financial risk.

- **Inventory Control,** similar to AR, has a direct impact on cash flow and short term payment capabilities. Inventory surpluses contribute to overstocks and loss of readily available cash. Inventory represents a current asset on the balance sheet but does tie up monies otherwise available for expenses and other purposes. Some companies opt to maintain larger inventories than are required to meet need; inasmuch their balance sheet's apparent profitability. Other costs to the organization in maintaining elevated amount of inventory include the resources need to store and insure the same. Businesses that stock too little inventory cannot take advantage of large orders from customers if they cannot deliver. Being able to quickly meet customer product needs and the costs associated with those needs are inherent challenges faced by managers.

Operational Challenges

An unfortunate reality for busy managers with multiple responsibilities is that cursory review of financial statements and ratios is routine, while diligent analysis fails in light of heavy responsibilities and information overload. Managers responsible for the financial performance of an organization often hold concurrent responsibility for managing the operations of the entity, finding themselves charged with appropriate and timely decision-making as well as with the handling of day to day crises. Inherent dangers for a manager applying insufficient focus on an operations' fiscal performance can include faulty and irresponsible economic decisions, which can result in internal misappropriation by employees and added complexity and cost resulting from delayed action on error or discrepancy of the "books." An article in "Accenture" reveals a shocking reality, "According to an article recently published by Capgemini, one in four decisions made by {UK} executives were wrong, costing an average of 800,000 pounds per year" (Barrett, 2003). The author directly relates the inaccuracy of decision-making to late (out of date) data or inaccuracies in the reported information. He goes on in his report, "Our own recent survey found that only 22% of managers know which products and customers are profitable at any point in time, while a quarter are making decisions intuitively" (Barrett, 2003).

Responsible financial management requires intensive drill-down beyond account balances and cash flow review to provide timely action and reaction to manipulate the entire spectrum of the company's financial performance. Management's diligence to these functions directly impacts the running of a business, the evaluation of departments and individuals, and strategic planning. In today's environment, as companies grow and consolidate, skillful managers are required take responsibility for elimination of redundancy, and identification of inherent weaknesses in existing systems. It cannot be overstated that implementation of internal controls and oversight are fundamental to the success of the business. Today, finance leaders are foolhardy if they are not acutely aware that holding a degree in accounting or an MBA and "being good with numbers" is no longer enough to guarantee success in key management positions. Ronald O. Reed, Professor of Accounting and Wall Street Journal Fellow, Monfort College of Business, reported in "Financial Executive" "the expanded roles of CFOs (Financial Managers) will require skills beyond technology accounting. They will be expected to have a skill set that will require them to identify, assess and monitor the risks. They will need problem resolution skills, communication skills and personnel skills. In short, the {role} will be expanded beyond the traditional reporting and internal control areas and into being the trusted financial advisor and risk manager" (Marshall, Heffes, 2006).

Case Study: Department of Homeland Security & Oversight

Real-life evidence of risks and losses resulting from insufficient oversight are readily found in the literature. Insufficient internal controls and financial management in government are prime examples of ever-present risk of fraud or delayed action. Business and financial managers must take heed and stay abreast of relevant issues that ultimately impact their business interests. For example, In July, 2007, the United States Government Accountability Office (GAO) issued a report on a financial integration review conducted on the Department of Homeland's Financial Systems Modernization Project. Reasons behind the review and recommendations to the agency were related to historical cross-departmental irresponsibility and lack of sufficient oversight to protect federal dollars. Among many deficiencies, the review found $677 million in inventory and supplies. This same report found "DHS had an inventory of over 500 financial management systems and had inherited 18 internal control weaknesses (GAO, 2007). Clearly, businesses cannot survive without diligent work and ongoing attention to daily operations and oversight of resources. Assembling the resources and expertise to accomplish objectives is often the number one challenge facing business today.

Recommendations for Department of Homeland Security

Improvements were and continue to be slow and challenging. Waste and redundancy in financial management plague this organization which has grown to suffer a complex and poorly-functioning accountability system. In the report, the following direction was given to the Department of Homeland Security leadership:

- Develop a concept of operations document
- Define standard business practices
- Development and implementation (and migration) strategy
- Define and effectively implement disciplined processes necessary to properly manage specific projects (US Government Accountability Office, 2007).

Frustration with identifying results-driven, leadership, inadequate accountability and vast complexity surround the department and highlight the challenges financial managers face in today's environment.

Discourse

Strictly defined, accounting is the measurement, disclosure or imparting of assurance about financial information primarily used by managers, investors, tax authorities and other decision makers to make resource allocation decisions within business entities. Business accounting follows Generally Accepted Accounting Principles (GAAP), to give outside stakeholders, such as creditors, consistent reporting methodologies for assessment of the company. GAAP rules govern everything from recognizing assets and liabilities to the notes attached to a financial statement (Womack, 2005). Public firms undergo accounting audits which render comment on their financial statements. Historically, accounting firms, such as Arthur Anderson, one of the "Big Five" accounting firms, self-regulated their auditing practices with no governmental requirements to defend their reviews.

Public vs. Private Oversight

Public organizations have long been subject to scrutiny of their financial practices, governed by legislators and stakeholders. Although federal requirements do not weigh as heavily on the private sector, it is within reason to expect that similarly stringent practices would be of value to non-public companies' executives. Discrepant levels of oversight between private and public companies can create confusion and inconsistency. Many private companies are modeling their financial oversight practices following recent federal legislation mandates.

Sarbanes Oxley Law

Legislation passed into law in July, 2002 by President Bush was in direct response to accounting scandals and public mistrust involving Enron, Tyco International and other major companies. The Federal Sarbanes Oxley Law (Sarbox) governs accountancy and financial oversight of public firms. The mandates driven by Sarbox are designed to strengthen reporting controls; their secondary benefit is to alleviate public fears that uncontrolled practices threaten the interests of the public owners.

Within the context of the Sarbox Law, the Public Company Accounting Oversight Board (PCAOB) was established; this entity's role is to oversee, regulate, review, inspect and discipline accounting firms serving as auditors in public companies. As referenced earlier, non-public organizations which do not have to comply with Sarbanes Oxley are opting to follow the regulations nonetheless. "Some private companies have chosen to comply with SOX even if they don't have to, either because they think they might be purchased by a public company, or go public themselves, or because they want better control over financial accounting" (Brodkin, 2007). Because implementation of more vigorous controls will inevitably increase expenses, some organizations are apt to maintain the status quo. It is the more risk-averse who are willing to make the investment because of perceived savings and "insurance" to the company. Stakeholders expect and in fact demand that those with governance responsibility of a company implement controls in their best financial interest.

The Raytheon Fraud Initiative

According to the Association of Fraud Examiners in Austin, Texas, 5% of United States companies' revenues were lost to fraud in 2006; approximately 652 billion dollars. One company, Raytheon, Incorporated, a defense and aerospace technology supplier based in Massachusetts, chose to embark on "an independent governance initiative" which brought to the organization an educational initiative to raise awareness about fraud in the company (Krell, 2007). Raytheon brought in external auditors from the accounting firm, Ernst and Young, who worked with managers throughout the organization to consider potential fraud scenarios potentially threatening the organization. The result of the effort reported not only a substantially heightened awareness but an improvement in communication and the ability to talk about such subjects as fraud that were previously considered uncomfortable for employees to discuss. According to the article in Business Finance, controls against fraud fall into place with simple routine assessments of operations such as:

- Routine assessment of budget variances
- Checking numbering discrepancies
- Reviewing for obvious tampering which becomes evident when management is paying close attention.

Raytheon's Action Plan included the following (Krell, 2007):

- Enlisting outside expertise collaboration
- Collaboration with business employees and managers
- Risk analysis; looking at likely fraud scenarios for their company
- Internal controls; preventative and detective to address potential fraud scenarios.

The Raytheon fraud initiative accomplished much more than originally conceived; it serves as an ideal example for new and experienced managers to continually focus on innovative thinking and a holistic manner of evaluating a company's business management as a system.

Conclusion

This article gives an introductory overview of the specific financial management functions and skill sets required of financial managers. As businesses expand, much more is at risk in terms of financial viability and growth opportunities unless exceptional individuals are recruited or grown for these positions. Complexity, growth and globalization present opportunities and threats to organizations every day. The future holds a great need for auditing personnel with technological expertise, strong internal company commitment, and multi-dimensional skill sets. Such individuals will be highly sought after in the coming years. Effective professionals who focus on staying current with industry changes and are strong in interpersonal and analytic skills will remain highly sought after in the coming years.

Terms & Concepts

Accounting Audit: The external review of a company's financial information and the internal examination of its financial records and related documentation.

Accounts Receivable: Business transactions dealing with the billing of customers who owe money to a business for goods or services sold on credit. The customers are generally invoiced with an expectation of payment to the business within the company's established timeframe.

Balance Sheet: A statement of the book value of all of the assets and liabilities (including equity) of a business or other organization or person at a particular date — a snapshot of the company's financial status on a given date.

Cash Flow Statement: A financial statement that shows a company's incoming and outgoing money during a specific time period (for example monthly or quarterly).

Controller (Comptroller): Person who oversees cash flow in a business entity. The controller may be a public official who holds responsibility for government account audits or is a Certified Public Accountant in a company.

External Review: The evaluation of an organization's financial information to ascertain the validity and reliability of information, this review is also to provide an assessment of a system's internal control.

Government Accountability Office (GAO): The audit, evaluation, and investigative arm of the United States Congress. The head of GAO is supposed to investigate, at the seat of government or elsewhere, all matters relating to the receipt, disbursement, and application of public funds.

Income Statement: An organization's Profit and Loss Statement (P & L), is a financial report for companies that indicates net income derived from the sale of products and services less related expenses during a specific period of time.

Information Systems (IS): The matrix of persons, data records and activities that process the data and information in a business organization. IS are commonly considered (erroneously) synonymous for computer-processed and provided information

Internal Oversight: Careful oversight of an organization's assets and financial activities to protect the interests of the organization and/or its stakeholders.

Inventory Control: The process of minimizing the total cost of inventory in order to diminish the amount of money tied up (not available as cash) in holding the product, including purchase costs, storage, management and insurance.

Raytheon, Inc.: Technology leader specializing in defense, homeland security, and other government markets throughout the world. With a history of innovation spanning more than 80 years, Raytheon provides state-of-the-art electronics, mission systems integration, and other capabilities in the areas of sensing; effects; command, control, communications and intelligence systems, as well as a broad range of mission support services (http://www.raytheon.com/about/).

Sarbanes Oxley: Legislation passed in 2002 which establishes new or enhanced standards for all U.S. public company boards, management, and public accounting firms.

Scorecard: A conceptual framework for measuring an organization's activities in the context of mission, vision and strategy; used to give managers a wide-ranging view of the performance of a business.

Bibliography

Balbi, A. (2013). IFAC's CFO Paper. *Strategic Finance, 95*(11), 24. Retrieved November 15, 2013, from EBSCO Online Database Business Source Complete. http://search.ebscohost.com/login.aspx?direct=true&db=bth&AN=91860244&site=ehost-live

Barrett, R. (2004). Invoice errors and inefficient tools put finance professionals under the spotlight. *Credit Control, 25*(8), 28-31. Retrieved August 28, 2007, from EBSCO Online Database Business Source Premier. http://search.ebscohost.com/login.aspx?direct=true&db=buh&AN=15841973&site=ehost-live

Brodkin, J. (2007). SOX: Five years of headaches. *Network World, 24*(29), 1-16. Retrieved August 29, 2007, from EBSCO Online Database Business Source Premier. http://search.ebscohost.com/login.aspx?direct=true&db=buh&AN=25985000&site=ehost-live

Goldstein, M. (1995). AICPA poll foresees sweeping changes in financial management functions. *CPA Journal, 65*(3), 68. Retrieved September 1, 2007, from EBSCO Online Database Business Source Premier. http://search.ebscohost.com/login.aspx?direct=true&db=buh&AN=9504270803&site=ehost-live

Homeland Security: Responses to post hearing questions related to the Department of Homeland Security's integrated financial management systems challenges: GAO-07-1157R. (2007, August 10). *GAO Reports*, 1-11. Retrieved September 2, 2007, from EBSCO Online Database Business Source Premier. http://search.ebscohost.com/login.aspx?direct=true&db=buh&AN=26299576&site=ehost-live

Krell, E. (2007). The Awakening. *Business Finance, 13*(8), 22-26. Retrieved September 2, 2007, from EBSCO Online Database Business Source Complete. http://search.ebscohost.com/login.aspx?direct=true&db=bth&AN=26225763&site=ehost-live

Marshall, J., & Heffes, E. (2006). What does the future hold, for finance and CFOs? *Financial Executive, 22*(10), 16-20. Retrieved September 1, 2007, from EBSCO Online Database Business Source Premier. http://search.ebscohost.com/login.aspx?direct=true&db=buh&AN=23331579&site=ehost-live

Riedl, E.J., & Srinivasan, S. (2010). Signaling firm performance through financial statement presentation: An analysis using special items. *Contemporary Accounting Research, 27*(1), 289-332. Retrieved November 15, 2013, from EBSCO Online Database Business Source Complete. http://search.ebscohost.com/login.aspx?direct=true&db=bth&AN=57556531&site=ehost-live

Shirur, S. (2013). Are managers measuring the financial risk in the right manner? An exploratory study. *Vikalpa: The Journal For Decision Makers, 38*(2), 81-94. Retrieved November 15, 2013, from EBSCO Online Database Business Source Complete. http://search.ebscohost.com/login.aspx?direct=true&db=bth&AN=89174332&site=ehost-live

Womack, B. (2005). Big GAAP: Private firms seek accounting fixes. *San Diego Business Journal, 26*(32), 21-21. Retrieved August 29, 2007, from EBSCO Online Database Health Business Full text Elite database. http://search.ebscohost.com/login.aspx?direct=true&db=heh&AN=18076598&site=ehost-live

Worth, J. (2013). One for the books. *Entrepreneur, 41*(1), 66. Retrieved November 15, 2013, from EBSCO Online Database Business Source Complete. http://search.ebscohost.com/login.aspx?direct=true&db=bth&AN=84366620&site=ehost-live

Suggested Reading

Brodkin, J. (2007). SOX: Five years of headaches. *Network World, 24*(29), 1-16. Retrieved August 27, 2007, from EBSCO Online Database Business Source Premier. http://search.ebscohost.com/login.aspx?direct=true&db=buh&AN=25985000&site=ehost-live

Financial management: Long-standing financial systems weaknesses present a formidable challenge: GAO-07-914. (2007, August 6). *GAO Reports*, 1-59. Retrieved August 25, 2007, from EBSCO Online Database Business Source Premier. http://search.ebscohost.com/login.aspx?direct=true&db=buh&AN=26165783&site=ehost-live

Internal controls — the value of a wider business-led approach. (2006). *CMA Management, 80*(7), 22-25. Retrieved August 29, 2007, from EBSCO Online Database Business Source Complete. http://search.ebscohost.com/login.aspx?direct=true&db=bth&AN=23497221&site=ehost-live

Van Wijk, E. (2005). Siphoning: the audit department. *Internal Auditor, 62*(3), 77-81. Retrieved September 2, 2007, from EBSCO Online Database Business Source Premier. http://search.ebscohost.com/login.aspx?direct=true&db=buh&AN=17479992&site=ehost-live

Wilkins, S., & Gupta, P. (2007). Sustaining SOX 404: A project management approach. *Management Accounting Quarterly, 8*(2), 1-14. Retrieved August 28, 2007, from EBSCO Online Database Business Source Premier. http://search.ebscohost.com/login.aspx?direct=true&db=buh&AN=24958027&site=ehost-live

Essay by Nancy Devenger

Nancy Devenger holds a BS degree from the University of New Hampshire and a Masters Degree in Health Policy from Dartmouth College's Center for the Evaluative and Clinical Sciences. Nancy began her career in health care as a registered nurse for many years. Since earning her undergraduate degree in Business, Nancy has worked in private medical practice, home health, consulting, and most currently as Director of Ambulatory Operations for a large Academic Medical Center. Her operational experience as a business manager in private medical practice and for the last decade in a tertiary medical center have allowed Nancy broad insight into both private and academic business endeavors.

Use of Managerial Economics in Finance

Table of Contents

Abstract
Overview
    Profits
    Wealth Maximization
Application
    Market Structures
Viewpoint
    Capital Budgeting
Conclusion
Terms & Concepts
Bibliography
Suggested Reading

Abstract

This article focuses on how financial professionals utilize managerial economics in making decisions to resolve business problems. Managerial economics highlights how financial professionals make decisions regarding resource allocation, strategic, and tactical issues that relate to all types of firms from an economic perspective. Profits and wealth maximization are key factors in managerial economics. Profits are very crucial to a firm's bottom line, and wealth maximization is a long term operational goal. Market structures take into consideration: The number of firms in an industry, the relative size of the firms (industry concentration), demand conditions, ease of entry and exit, and technological and cost conditions.

Overview

Managerial economics highlights how financial professionals make decisions regarding resource allocation, strategic, and tactical issues that relate to all types of firms from an economic perspective. These professionals use a series of techniques in order to find the most efficient way to reach the best decisions for the firm. The major emphasis is to provide the analytical tools and managerial insights essential to the analyses and solutions of those problems that have significant economic consequences, both for the firm and for the world economy.

Managerial economics occurs when the fundamental principles of microeconomics is applied in the decision making process of business and managerial problems. It can be applied to problems in private, public and non-profit organizations. According to Skim and Siegel (1998), the basic steps in the decision making process are:

- **Recognize and define the problem.** Once a problem has been identified, an exact statement describing the problem should be prepared.

- **Select a goal.** Is it profit maximizing or cost minimizing?

- **Identify any constraints.** All possible constraints need to be identified.

- **Identify alternatives or define decision variables a firm is trying to solve for.**

- **Select the alternative consistent with the firm's objectives or determine the optimal solution** (i.e. profit-maximizing or cost-minimizing solution), p. 3.

Managerial economics connects the practical and theoretical aspects of economics. Many economists will utilize a variety of techniques from other business fields such as finance and operations management. Most business decisions can be analyzed with the techniques used in managerial economics. However, it is most often used in:

- **Risk Analysis** Assorted uncertainty models, decision guidelines, and risk quantification methods help to interpret how much risk is involved in a given arrangement of decision.

- **Production Analysis** Microeconomics methods help to assess the effectiveness of production, the best factor distribution, the costs involved, the frugality of scale and the company's estimated cost function.

- **Pricing Analysis** — Microeconomic methods facilitate the analysis of multiple pricing options that involve trans-

fer costs, joint product costs, cost discrimination, cost elasticity approximations, and deciding upon the right pricing technique for the job.
- **Capital Budgeting** — Investment theory allows for the examination of a corporation's capital purchasing decision.

Managerial economics is "the systematic studies of how resources should be allocated in such a way to most efficiently achieve a managerial goal" (Shim & Siegel, 1998, p. 2).

Profits

Profits are very crucial to a firm's bottom line. When a firm is able to make a profit, there is an assumption that the company has done a good job of effectively and efficiently in controlling cost while producing a quality product or performing a quality service. However, there are different types of profits. Two types of profits are accounting profits and economic profits. Accounting profits are determined by the difference between the total revenue and the cost of producing products or services, and they appear on the firm's income statement. Economic profits are determined by the difference between total revenue and the total opportunity costs. The opportunity costs tend to be higher than accounting and bookkeeping costs.

Profits tend to vary across industries, and there are a number of theories that attempt to provide an explanation as to why this occurs. Five of the most discussed theories in this area are:

- Risk-Bearing Theory. When the owners of a company make investments into the firm, they take on a certain amount of risk. In order to compensate them for their investment, the company will need to have an above average return on economic profits. An example would be a firm that has investors such as venture capitalists or angel investors.
- Dynamic Equilibrium Theory. Every firm should strive to have a normal rate of profit. However, each firm has the opportunity to earn returns above or below the normal level at any time.
- Monopoly Theory. There are times when one firm may have the opportunity to dominate in its industry and earn above normal rates of return over a long period of time. These firms tend to dominate the market as a result of economies of scale, control of essential natural resources, control of crucial patents and/or government restrictions. An example would be utility companies.
- Innovation Theory. A firm may earn above normal profits as a reward for its successful innovations, such as patents. An example would be a pharmaceutical organization such as Astra Zeneca.
- Managerial Efficiency Theory. A firm may be able to earn above average profits based on its strong leadership team. This type of organization gains profits as a result of being effective and efficient. An example would be General Electric under Jack Welch's leadership.

Wealth Maximization

Wealth maximization is a long term operational goal. Shareholders have a residual claim on the firm's net cash flows after expected contractual claims have been paid. All other stakeholders (i.e. employers, customers) have contractual expected returns. There tends to be a preference for wealth maximization because it takes into consideration (Shim & Siegel, 1998):

- Wealth for the long term
- Risk or uncertainty
- The timing of returns
- The stockholders' return.

Criterion for this goal suggests that a firm should review and assess the expected profits and or cash flows as well as the risks that are associated with them. When conducting this evaluation, there are three points to keep in mind. First, economic profits are not equivalent to accounting profits. Second, accounting profits are not the same as cash flows. Lastly, financial analysis must focus on maximization of the present value of cash flows to the owners of the firm when attempting to maximize shareholder wealth.

When making decisions, the financial management team has to anticipate certain factors and realize that they may not have control over some of them. Factors outside of their control tend to be ones that are a part of the economic environment.

- Factors under administrative command
- Products and services made available
- Production technology
- Marketing and distribution
- Investment plans of action
- Employment policies and compensation
- Ownership form
- Capital structure
- Successful capital management tactics
- Dividend policies
- Alliances, mergers, spinoffs
- Factors not under management control
- Level of economic activity
- Tax rates and regulations
- Competition
- Laws and government regulations
- Unionization of employees
- International business conditions and currency exchange rates

In order for wealth maximization to be at the optimal level, certain conditions need to be in place. The process has a good chance to be successful when:

- **Complete markets are secure.** Liquid markets are needed for the firm's inputs, products and by-products.
- **There is no asymmetric information.** Buyers and sellers have the same information and no information is hidden from either group.
- **All re-contracting costs are known.** Managers know or expect the exact impending input costs as a portion of the current worth of anticipated cash flows.

When one reviews the wealth maximization model, there are some basic assumptions made about how the financial management team should respond. Some recommendations include:

- Develop a dynamic long term vision/outlook.
- Anticipate and manage change.
- Secure strategic investment opportunities.
- Maximize the present value of expected cash flows to owners.

In order to account for timing, future cash flows must be discounted by an interest rate that represents the cost of the funds being used to finance the project. Financial analysts have found the time value of money to be an important factor when making decisions on projects. Present value is the value today of future cash flows, and the computation of present values (discounting) is the opposite of determining the compounded future value. The discounted cash flow (DCF) analysis is a tool that tends to be used to account for the timing of cash inflows and outflows.

The purpose of using the DCF analysis is to get an estimate of how much money can be gained by investing in a specific project. An adjustment for the time value of money is also taken into consideration. DCF analysis uses the weighted average cost of capital to discount future free cash flow projections in order to get the present value. Once the present value has been determined, it is used by financial analysts to determine whether or not a project is a potential investment. Good prospects are those projects in which the DCF analysis is higher than the current cost of the project investment. Currently, there are four different DCF methods utilized. The type of method utilized is determined based on the financing schedule of the firm. The four methods fall into two categories — equity approach and entity approach. The "flows to equity approach" falls under the equity approach. There are three methods under the entity approach, they are: The adjusted present value approach, weighted average cost of capital approach and the total cash flow approach.

However, there are some pitfalls with using the DCF analysis. Harman (2007) pointed out three potential problems with DCF.

- **Operating Cash Flow Projections** "The first and most important factor in calculating the DCF value of a stock is estimating the series of operating cash flow projections. There are a number of problems with earnings and cash flow forecasting that can generate problems with DCF analysis. The most prevalent is that the uncertainty with cash flow projection increases for each year in the forecast, and DCF models often use five or even 10 years' worth of estimates" (Harman, 2007, "Problems with DCF"). Analysts might be able to estimate what the operating cash flow will be for that year and the impending year. But, the projecting earnings and cash flow becomes more compromised as time progresses. Cash flow projections for a certain year will also weigh heavily on the recorded results from past years. Small, incorrect estimations during the first few years of a model can dramatically increase any differences in cash flow projections that are made down the road.

- **Capital Expenditure Projections** "Free cash flow projection involves projecting capital expenditures for each model year. The degree of uncertainty increases with each additional year in the model. Capital expenditures can be largely discretionary. In a down year, a firm may elect to reduce capital expenditure plans since they tend to be risky. While there are a number of techniques to calculate capital expenditures, such as using fixed asset turnover ratios or even a percentage of revenues method, small changes in model assumptions can widely affect the result of the DCF calculation" (Harman, 2007, "Problems with DCF").

- **Discount Rate and Growth Rate** "There are many ways to approach the discount rate in an equity DCF model. Analysts might use the Markowitzian R = Rf + ? (Rm - Rf) or the weighted average cost of capital of the firm as the discount rate in the DCF model. Both approaches are quite theoretical and may not work well in real world investing applications" (Harman, 2007, "Problems with DCF"). Other methods involve choosing to use an "arbitrary standard hurdle rate" to estimate and assess each equity investment. Such a technique lets each investment be analyzed alongside the others. It is often hard to choose a particular estimating technique for discount rates that is both accurate and concise.

Application

Market Structures

Market structures take into consideration:

- The number of firms in an industry
- The relative size of the firms (industry concentration)
- Demand conditions
- Ease of entry and exit
- Technological and cost conditions.

The preferred structure is dependent on the type of industry. Therefore, the financial management team of each firm determines which of the above-mentioned factors will be a part of the decision making process.

The level of competition tends to be dependent on whether there are many (or a few) firms in the industry and if the firm's products are similar or different. Given this information, four basic approaches to market structure and the types of competition have been established.

- **Perfect (Pure) Competition** (Many sellers of a standardized product) Characteristics of perfect competition are:
  - Large number of buyers and sellers
  - Homogeneous product
  - Complete knowledge
  - Easy entry and exit from the market.

A firm using this approach tends to be small relative to the total market, and it will offer its product at the going market price. A firm in this format operates at an output level where price (or marginal revenue) is equal to the marginal cost and profit maximized. This format is more theoretical because there is no firm that operates at this level.

- **Monopolistic Competition** (Many sellers of a differentiated product)

Characteristics of monopolistic competition are: One firm, no close substitutes, no interdependence among firms, and substantial barriers to entry. In addition, there tends to be many buyers and sellers, there is product differentiation, easy entry and exit and independent decision making by individual firms. An example of a firm fitting this profile would be a small business selling differentiated, yet similar, products. These firms will utilize three basic strategies in order to obtain their principal goal of maximum profits: Price changes, variations in the products, and promotional activities.

- **Oligopoly** (Few sellers of either a standardized or a differentiated product)

Characteristics of an oligopoly are (1) few firms, (2) high degree of interdependence among firms; (3) product may be homogenous or differentiated, and (4) difficult entry and exit from market. The market fits this approach when there are a small number of firms supplying the dominant share of an industry's total output. Oligopolists are interdependent based on all levels of competition — price, output, promotional strategies, customer service policies, acquisitions and mergers, etc. Therefore, decision makers may have a hard time anticipating what rivals will do in reaction to their position, which makes the process complex. Two popular models are Cournot's duopoly model and kinked demand curve. An example would be the NCAA. This organization controls the revenues and costs of its member schools. It has the power to limit the number of games and times that a school can have its games televised. The NCAA retains control over costs through its restrictions on the compensation of student athletes.

- **Monopoly** (A single seller of a product for which there is no close substitute)

A monopoly occurs when one firm produces a highly differentiated product in a market with significant barriers to entry. It may be large or small, and it must be the only supplier. In addition, there are not any similar substitutes available. Since the monopoly is the only producer, it is known as the industry, while its demand curve is called the industry demand. An example would be an electric utility company in a specific geographic area.

What is the difference between the monopoly and pure approach? A profit-maximizing monopoly firm will produce less and charge a higher price than firms collectively in a purely competitive industry. However, both demand and cost may be different for a monopoly firm (i.e. a monopoly may be able to take advantage of economies of scale).

Viewpoint

Capital Budgeting

Many organizations charge the finance department with overseeing the financial stability of the firm. The chief financial officer (CFO) may lead a team of financial analysts to determine which projects deserve investment. "The economic theory of the firm suggests that to maximize its profit, a firm should operate at the point where the marginal cost of an additional unit of output just equals the marginal revenue derived from that output, and this may be equally applicable to the capital budgeting process" (Shim & Siegel, 1998, p. 279). Capital budgeting is an example of how a firm may conduct a cost-benefit analysis. There is a comparison between the cash inflows (benefits) and outflows (costs) in order to determine which is greater. Capital budgeting could be the result of purchasing assets that are new for the firm or getting rid of some of the current assets in order to be more efficient. The finance team will be charged with evaluating (1) which projects would be good investments, (2) which assets would add value to the current portfolio, and (3) how much the firm is willing to invest into each asset.

In order to answer questions about potential assets, there are a set of components to be considered in the capital budgeting process. The four components are: Initial investment outlay, net cash benefits (or savings) from the operations, terminal cash flow, and net present value (NPV) technique. "Capital budgeting is a financial analysis tool that applies quantitative analysis to support strong management decisions" (Bearing Point, n.d.).

Capital budgeting seeks to provide a simple way for the finance department to see the "big picture" of the benefits, costs and risks for a corporation planning to make short term and/or long term investments. Unfortunately, many of the leading methods have experienced problems, especially when a firm is using a standardized template. Examples of potential problems include:

The benefits, costs, and risks associated with an investment tend to be different based on the type of industry (i.e. technological versus agricultural).

A corporation may highlight the end results of the return on investment model and the assumptions that support the results versus a balanced analysis of benefits, costs, and risks.

If a firm does not account for the above-mentioned scenarios, there is a possibility of the results being skewed, which would make the data unusable. This type of error could hinder a project from getting approved. Therefore, it is critical for financial analysts to have a more effective and efficient technique to use. Bearing Point (n.d.) identified several leading practices that organizations are using in order to avoid reporting faulty information. The theme in all of the techniques is that capital budgeting is not the only factor considered. Other quantifiable factors are utilized in order to see the big picture.

Consider the nature of the request — The type of benefit obtained by the investment will determine the nature of the request. Therefore, it may be beneficial to classify the benefit types into categories such as strategic, quantifiable and intangible.

All benefits are not created equal — Benefits should be classified correctly in order to properly analyze them. There are two types of benefits — hard and soft. Hard benefits affect the profit and loss statement directly, but soft benefits do not have the same affect.

Quantify risk — Make sure that the risks are properly evaluated. In most cases, risks are neglected. Also, it would be a good idea to build a risk factor into whatever model is utilized.

Be realistic about benefit periods. Make sure that the expectations are realistic. In the past, corporations have created unrealistic goals for the benefits period by (1) anticipating benefits to come too early and (2) reusing models that reflect the depreciation period for the capital asset.

Conclusion

Managerial economics highlights how financial professionals make decisions regarding resource allocation, strategic, and tactical issues that relate to all types of firms from an economic perspective. Managerial economics occurs when the fundamental principles of microeconomics are applied to the decision making process of business and managerial problems. It can apply to problems in private, public and non-profit organizations. Managerial economics connects the practical and theoretical aspects of economics. Many economists will utilize a variety of techniques from other business fields such as finance and operations management.

Profits are very crucial to a firm's bottom line. There are two types of profits — accounting profits and economic profits. Profits tend to vary across industries, and there are a number of theories that attempt to provide an explanation as to why this occurs.

Wealth maximization is a long term operational goal. There tends to be a preference for wealth maximization because it takes into consideration (1) wealth for the long term, (2) risk or uncertainty, (3) the timing of returns, and (4) the stockholders' return (Shim & Siegel, 1998). "The economic theory of the firm suggests that to maximize its profit, a firm should operate at the point where the marginal cost of an additional unit of output just equals the marginal revenue derived from that output, and this may be equally applicable to the capital budgeting process" (Shim & Siegel, 1998, p. 279). Capital budgeting is an example of how a firm may conduct a cost-benefit analysis.

Terms & Concepts

Accounting Profits: The difference between the total revenue and the cost of producing goods or services.

Capital Budgeting: The process of choosing certain long-term projects that are worthy of undertaking and investment. The potential projects are usually chosen based on their prospective discounted cash flows and the internal rates of return.

Discounted Cash Flow Analysis: A valuation method used to estimate the attractiveness of an investment opportunity.

Economic Profits: The difference between the total revenue and the total opportunity costs.

Managerial Economics: The branch of economics applied in managerial decision making.

Present Value Analysis: The evaluation of the current value of impending payments that are discounted at the rate R, which is known as the current bank balance that is paying interest at the rate R that is necessary in order to accurately imitate the future payment values.

Pricing Analysis: Microeconomic methods that are utilized in order to assess different pricing decisions.

Production Analysis: Microeconomic methods that help to assess production effectiveness, the best factor allocation, the costs, the benefits of scale, and the estimation of the company's cost function.

Profit Maximization: A hypothesis that the goal of a firm is to maximize its profit.

Risk Analysis: Assessing the extent of risk of a decision based on different uncertainty models, decision rules, and methods of risk quantification.

Time Value of Money: The concept that money available now has higher value than it will at the same amount in the future based on its potential earning capability. Assuming that money is likely to earn interest, any amount of dollars is more heavily weighted the sooner it is received. This concept is also known as "present discounted value."

Wealth Maximization: In an efficient market, it is the maximization of the current share price.

Bibliography

Andreae, C.A. (1970). The study of finance as a management science. *Management International Review (MIR), 10*(1), 87-99. Retrieved November 15, 2013, from EBSCO Online Database Business Source Complete. http://search.ebscohost.com/login.aspx?direct=true&db=bth&AN=12253215&site=ehost-live

Bearing Point (n.d.). Improve your capital budget techniques. Retrieved July 9, 2007, from http://office.microsoft.com/en-us/help/HA011553851033.aspx

Harman, B. (2007, July 9). Top three DCF analysis pitfalls. Retrieved July 28, 2007, from http://www.investopedia.com/articles/07/DCF%5fpitfalls.asp.

McGuigan, J., Moyer, C., & Harris, F. (2007). *Managerial economics: Applications, strategies, and tactics.* Southwestern Publishing.

Mintz, O., & Currim, I.S. (2013). What drives managerial use of marketing and financial metrics and does metric use affect performance of marketing-mix activities?. *Journal of Marketing, 77*(2), 17-40. Retrieved November 15, 2013, from EBSCO Online Database Business Source Complete. http://search.ebscohost.com/login.aspx?direct=true&db=bth&AN=85725800&site=ehost-live

Shim, J., & Siegel, J. (1998). *Managerial economics.* New York: Barron's Educational Series, Inc.

Suggested Reading

Block, W. (2001). Cyberslacking, business ethics and managerial economics. *Journal of Business Ethics, Part 1, 33*(3), 225-231. Retrieved July 25, 2007, from EBSCO Online Database Business Source Complete. http://search.ebscohost.com/login.aspx?direct=true&db=bth&AN=5440168&site=ehost-live

Cafferata, R. (1997). Nonprofit organizations privatization and the mixed economy: A managerial economics perspective. *Annals of Public & Cooperative Economics, 68*(4), 665-689. Retrieved July 25, 2007, from EBSCO Online Database Business Source Complete. http://search.ebscohost.com/login.aspx?direct=true&db=bth&AN=4491985&site=ehost-live

Guiffrida, A., & Nagi, R. (2006). Economics of managerial neglect in supply chain delivery performance. *Engineering Economist, 51*(1), 1-17. Retrieved July 25, 2007, from EBSCO Online Database Business Source Complete. http://search.ebscohost.com/login.aspx?direct=true&db=bth&AN=19906612&site=ehost-live

Essay by Marie Gould

Marie Gould is an Associate Professor and the Faculty Chair of the Business Administration Department at Peirce College in Philadelphia, Pennsylvania. She teaches in the areas of management, entrepreneurship, and international business. Although Ms. Gould has spent her career in both academia and corporate, she enjoys helping people learn new things — whether it's by teaching, developing or mentoring.

Financial Information Systems

Table of Contents

Abstract

Overview

    Components of Accounting Information Systems

    Choosing the Appropriate System

    The Foreign Corrupt Practices Act

    Financial Accounting

    The Financial Accounting Audit Trail

    The Nine Steps of the Accounting Cycle

Application

    Financial Management Information Systems

    Characteristics of Financial Management Information Systems

    Characteristics of a Well Designed Financial Management Information System

Viewpoint

    FMIS in Developing Countries

    The Four-Step FMIS Creation Process for Developing Countries

Conclusion

Terms & Concepts

Bibliography

Suggested Reading

Abstract

This article focuses on the financial accounting process and the benefits of automating the process. The financial accounting process is defined and each step of the financial accounting cycle is explained. The accounting department is a key player in an organization's ability to be successful. This department is responsible for providing information to internal and external entities so that they can make effective financial decisions that will benefit the organization. These decisions will have a profound effect on the organization so it is imperative that the data collected is accurate.

Overview

The accounting department is a key player in an organization's ability to succeed. This department is responsible for providing information to internal and external entities so that they can make effective financial decisions that will benefit the organization. These decisions will have a profound effect on the organization so it is imperative that the data collected is accurate. One way to ensure that the data is accurate is to install an accounting information system (AIS).

An accounting information system (AIS) is a system that records an organization's financial data and transactions. This information consists of the organization's revenues and expenditures as well as other financial transactions. A business will implement an AIS in order to accumulate data so that those responsible for making decisions have a supply of information over a period of time.

Components of Accounting Information Systems

Most accounting information systems have two components — financial and managerial accounting. The objective of financial accounting is to provide information to external decision makers, whereas, the objective of managerial accounting is to provide information to internal decision makers. Although both areas need to use an organization's accounting records, there are differences between the two areas of accounting.

	Managerial Accounting	Financial Accounting
Primary User	Internal decision makers	External decision makers
Time Focus	Present and future	Historical
Organizational Focus	Segmented	Aggregate
Time Span of Reports	As needed	Quarterly and annually
Rules and Regulations	Does not need to follow GAAP	Mandatory to follow GAAP
Record-keeping	Formal or informal	Formal

Choosing the Appropriate System

An organization's management team has the ability to create any type of internal accounting system. However, cost may be a key factor in deciding what type of system will be selected. The type and amount of information that needs to be stored is another factor in selecting the most appropriate information system.

The Foreign Corrupt Practices Act

Both financial and managerial accounting is bound by the Foreign Corrupt Practices Act. This act is a "U.S. law forbidding bribery and other corrupt practices, and requiring that accounting records be maintained in reasonable detail and accuracy, and that an appropriate system of internal accounting be maintained" (Horngreen, Stratton, & Sundem, 2002, p. 7). In summary, Drury (1996) stated that managerial accounting focuses on the provision of information to people within the organization so that they can make better decisions, whereas, financial accounting emphasizes the need of an organization having the ability to provide financial information to stakeholders outside of the organization.

One of the main objectives of financial accounting is to be able to process an organization's financial transactions in an effective manner in order to produce accurate financial statements, such as income statements and balance sheets (Moscove & Simkin, 1981). Managerial accounting has three main areas of operation: Cost accounting, budgeting and systems study.

Financial Accounting

Financial accounting focuses on preparing financial statements for external decision-makers such as banks and government agencies. The primary purpose of the field is to review and monitor an organization's financial performance and report the results of the evaluation to potential stakeholders. Financial accountants are expected to create financial statements based on Generally Accepted Accounting Principles (GAAP). Financial accounting exists in order to: Produce general purpose financial statements, provide information to decision makers in the accounting field, and meet regulatory requirements.

The Financial Accounting Audit Trail

The basic inputs of the financial accounting structure are transactions that measure money. Organizations should be able to conduct an audit trail of their accounting transactions. This audit trail will show the flow of data that moves through the accounting information system. The financial accounting audit trail consists of inputs, processing and outputs. Inputs consist of documents such as sales invoices and payroll time cards, whereas, the outputs are final documents such as financial statements and other external reports. Processing will go from the input phase to the output phase. Steps taken in between these two points include: Recording journal entries, posting the entries to a general ledger, and preparing a trial balance from the general ledger account balances. Processing these transactions is considered to be a part of an organization's accounting cycle, which has nine steps.

The Nine Steps of the Accounting Cycle

According to Moscove & Simkins (1985), the nine steps in the accounting cycle are:

- Prepare transaction source documents. Any type of transaction that causes a change in assets, liability, or owners' equity must be accounted for through documentation. Business transactions are the result of source documents being created. For example, the sales invoice represents a transaction source document (also referred to as an original record). Source documents are visual representation that a transaction exists. Many corporations will have a policy indicating that a financial transaction cannot be entered into its accounting information system until the proper source documents are prepared and approved. Other common forms of source documents include purchase invoices, receiving reports, bills of lading, employee time cards, and voucher checks.

- Sourcing documents allow an organization to collect its transaction data for subsequent entry into the accounting information system. In addition, transaction source documents act as the starting point in an organization's audit trail flow of data through its information system's accounting cycle.

- Recording business transactions in a journal. Once the accounting data has been collected, it is recorded in the organization's journal. Many organizations will maintain a journal within an accounting information system in order to keep a chronological record of the activities that have occurred throughout its lifecycle. There are large amounts of transactions that need to be processed. Therefore, many organizations will switch from a manual system to a computerized financial information system. The computerized system can provide a more efficient approach to tracking the various categories that will occur when the company is performing business transactions. Some of the most common categories are: Assets, operating expenses, the sale of products and/or services, and the receipt and payment of cash.

- Posting business transactions from the journal to the general ledger and determining individual account balances. The general ledger contains detailed information about the organization's assets, liabilities, owners' equity, revenue and expenses. A "T" account is created for each type of monetary item in the organization. In order for an organization's management team to have the appropriate information, the individual debits and credits from journal entries must be transferred from their proper accounts within the general ledger. This process is called posting. Once the posting process has been completed, managers can determine the balance of each general ledger.

- Preparing a trial balance. Each organization determines when it wants to prepare financial statements. Common timeframes include annually, quarterly and monthly. Based on the established timeframe, all of the posting work must be completed by the designated time so that the value of each general ledger can be determined. Once the information is computed, the trial balance is prepared. The trial balance highlights all of the general ledger accounts together with their end of period balances. In addition, the trial balance (1) determines whether the total debit and total credit account balances equal one another and (2) prepares the financial statements for the organization.

- Recording adjusting entries in a journal. Before one can prepare the organization's financial statements, adjustments (adjusting journal entries) may need to be made. The need to adjust is based on the periodicity principle and the matching principle. In addition, there are four major types of adjusting entries at the end of the organization's accounting period. The major types are unrecorded expenses, unrecorded revenues, deferred expenses or prepaid expenses and deferred revenues.

- Posting adjusting journal entries to the general ledger, determining updated general ledger account balances and preparing an adjusted trial balance. An adjusted trial balance must be prepared before the organization can prepare its income statement and balance sheet. The purpose of preparing the second trial balance is to determine if the debit and credit account balances are still equal once the adjusting entry process has been completed.

- Preparing financial statements from adjusted trial balance. The organization will use the adjusted trial balance to prepare its financial statements.

- Recording closing entries in a journal, posting them to the general ledger and determining new balances of those accounts affected by closing entries.

- An organization will record and post closing entries in order to eliminate its individual revenue and expense account balances and transfer the net income into the owner's equity account. Organizations should prepare financial statements immediately after the close of its accounting period so that the information is available to its decision makers.

- Preparing a post-closing trial balance. Once the closing entries are journalized and posted, all of the revenue and expense accounts will have zero balances and the owners' equity capital accounts will have the current period's net income or loss. Once this information has been confirmed, a post-closing trial balance will be conducted in order to verify that the accounts with debit balances equal the accounts with credit balances. This is the final step.

Application

Financial Management Information Systems

Characteristics of Financial Management Information Systems

A financial management information system (FMIS) is a system that computerizes the public expenditure management process. According to Diamond and Khemani (2006), some of the characteristics of this type of system are:

- **It is a management tool.** A FMIS should cater to the needs of the management team, and be a tool that supports change.

- **It should provide a wide range of nonfinancial and financial information.** It should provide information that will assist the managers in making decisions. Also, the system should be imbedded in the government accounting system as well as be able to collect data on nonfinancial areas such as employee information, performance based budgets and types of goods and services produced.

- **It is a system.** The system should be able to connect, collect, process and provide data to all essential personnel in the budget system on a regular basis. Thus, all key personnel should have access to the system so that they can perform their designated duties.

The core components of a FMIS are general ledger, budgetary accounting, accounts payable, and accounts receivable. The non-core components are payroll system, budget development, procurement, project ledger, and asset module.

Characteristics of a Well Designed Financial Management Information System

According to Diamond and Khemani (2006), a well designed FMIS should:

- "Be modular, and capable of progressive upgrading to cater to future needs."

- "Offer a common platform and user interface to the stakeholders in different agencies responsible for financial management, for adding to and accessing the information database."

- "Maintain a historical database of budget and expenditure plans; transaction data at the highest level of detail; cash flows and bank account operations including checks issued, cancelled, and paid; cash balances, and; floats."
- "Have dedicated modules to handle monthly, rolling, short-term and long-term forward estimates of revenues, expenditures prepared by agencies, and corresponding estimates of the resulting cash flows."
- "Compile formal government accounts from the database of authorization and cash allocations, primary revenue and expenditure transactions of the agencies; and treasury operations, avoiding the need to duplicate data entry for accounting purposes."
- "Enable real-time reconciliation of parallel and related streams of transaction data."
- "Be flexible enough to provide user defined management information, aggregated at the desired level of detail from the database" (Diamond & Khemani, 2006).

Viewpoint

FMIS in Developing Countries

In most developing countries in the early 21st century, the budget and accounting process was either completed manually or with outdated software applications. As a result, their output was often unreliable and untimely. This created a concern when they needed to conduct budget planning, monitoring, expenditure control and reporting.

> "Further, governments have found it difficult to provide an accurate, complete, and transparent account of their financial position to Parliament or to other interested parties, including donors and the general public. This lack of information has hindered transparency and the enforcement of accountability in government, and has only contributed to the perceived governance problems in many of these countries" (Diamond & Khemani, 2006, p. 98).

In order to overcome these problems, many developing countries have adopted financial management information systems in order to be more effective and efficient in the accounting reporting process. Additionally, as global markets became both more open and more competitve, by 2011 more than 120 countries moved to adopt the International Financial Reporting Standards (IFRS). High-quality financial reporting was seen as necessary to attract foreign investment and increase domestic surpluses and economic growth rates (Lasmin, 2012).

The Four-Step FMIS Creation Process for Developing Countries

Diamond and Khemani (2006) devised a four step process for developing countries to introduce a FMIS.

Step 1: Preparatory
- "Preliminary concept design including an institutional and organizational assessment.
- Analysis of the key problem areas and ongoing reform programs.
- Feasibility study.
- Design project and draft project proposal.
- Formal approval of the project — securing government approval and donors' funding" (Diamond & Khemani, 2006).

Step 2: Design
- "Develop functional specification.
- Outline information technology (IT) strategy, including hardware and organizational issues.
- Prepare tender documents" (Diamond & Khemani, 2006).

Step 3: Procurement
- "Issue tenders for hardware and software and associated requirements.
- Evaluation of bids and award contract" (Diamond & Khemani, 2006).

Step 4: Implementation
- "Configuration analysis and specification of any additional IT, infrastructure, and communication requirements.
- Detailed business process and gap analysis mapping required functionality to package and identifying and specifying detailed parameterization, customization, procedural changes.
- Agreed customization and configuration of the system.
- Determine training needs and conduct training of personnel.
- Pilot run — parallel run of the system; resolve initial problems and evaluate system performance for roll-out.
- Roll out system to other ministries and agencies.
- Phased implementation of additional modules.
- Strengthening of internal system support and phasing out of consultant/contractor support" ((Diamond & Khemani, 2006, p 104).

Conclusion

The accounting department is a key player in an organization's ability to be successful. This department is responsible for providing information to internal and external entities so that they can make effective financial decisions that will benefit the organization. These decisions will have a profound effect on the organization so it is imperative that the data collected is accurate. One way to ensure that the data is accurate is to install an accounting information system (AIS).

Most accounting information systems have two components — financial and managerial accounting. The objective of financial accounting is to provide information to external decision makers, whereas, the objective of managerial accounting is to provide information to internal decision makers. Another objective of financial accounting is to process an organization's financial transactions in an effective manner in order to produce accurate financial statements, such as income statements and balance sheets (Moscove & Simkin, 1981).

A financial management information system (FMIS) is a system that computerizes the public expenditure management process. According to Khemani & Diamond (2006), the core components of a FMIS are general ledger, budgetary accounting, accounts payable, and accounts receivable. The non-core components are payroll system, budget development, procurement, project ledger, and asset module.

In most developing countries, the budget and accounting process is either completed manually or with outdated software applications. As a result, their output has been unreliable and not timely. Therefore, many have sought to implement a FMIS. This type of project should be viewed as a long term endeavor, and there should be a strong commitment to the project's successful completion.

Terms & Concepts

Accounting Information System: An organization's chronological list of debits and credits.

Audit Trail: A record of transactions in an information system that provides verification of the activity of the system.

Financial Accounting: Reporting of the financial position of an organization to external stakeholders.

Generally Accepted Accounting Principles (GAAP): Established by the Financial Accounting Standards Board, is a set of procedures and rules for compiling and recording financial information.

Managerial Accounting: Financial reporting that is aimed at helping managers to make decisions.

Matching Principle: Also known as the hedging principle or cash flow matching approach, refers to the process of balancing an organization's assets with its liabilities; allows cash outflows to match cash inflows.

Periodicity Principle: Occurring at regular intervals.

Source Document: In finance, a document such as a purchase order, sales invoice or time card which provides original information on accounting transactions.

Trial Balance: Act of confirming that an organization's total debits equal the total credits; done by totaling both figures.

Bibliography

Al-Laith, A. (2012). Adaptation of the internal control systems with the use of information technology and its effects on the financial statements reliability: an applied study on commercial banks. *International Management Review, 8*(1), 12-20. Retrieved October 31, 2013, from EBSCO Online Database Business Source Complete. http://search.ebscohost.com/login.aspx?direct=true&db=bth&AN=75500334&site=ehost-live

Drury, C. (1996). *Management and cost accounting* (4th ed.). London: International Thompson Business Press.

Diamond, J., & Khemani, P. (2006). Introducing financial management information systems in developing countries. *OECD Journal on Budgeting, 5*(3), 98-132. Retrieved July 25, 2007, from EBSCO Online Database Business Source Complete. http://search.ebscohost.com/login.aspx?direct=true&db=bth&AN=21777790&site=ehost-live

Eccles, R.G., & Armbrester, K. (2011). Integrated reporting in the cloud. *IESE Insight,* (8), 13-20. Retrieved October 31, 2013, from EBSCO Online Database Business Source Complete. http://search.ebscohost.com/login.aspx?direct=true&db=bth&AN=60227579&site=ehost-live

Horngreen, C. T., Stratton, W. O., & Sundem, G. L. (2002). *Introduction to management accounting* (12th ed.). New Jersey: Prentice Hall.

Lasmin. (2012). Culture and the globalization of the international financial reporting standards (IFRS) in developing countries. *Journal of International Business Research,* 1131-44. Retrieved October 31, 2013, from EBSCO Online Database Business Source Complete. http://search.ebscohost.com/login.aspx?direct=true&db=bth&AN=85227515&site=ehost-live

Moscove, S., & Simkin, M. (1981). *Accounting information systems: Concepts and practice for effective decision making.* New York: John Wiley & Sons.

Suggested Reading

Burrowes, A. (2005). Core concepts of accounting information systems. *Issues in Accounting Education, 20*(2), 216-217. Retrieved July 25, 2007, from EBSCO Online Database Business Source Premier. http://search.ebscohost.com/login.aspx?direct=true&db=bth&AN=17022718&site=ehost-live

Bushman, R., Chen, Q., Engel, E., & Smith, A. (2004, June). Financial accounting information, organizational complexity and corporate governance systems. Journal of Accounting & Economics, 37(2), 167-201. Retrieved July 25, 2007, from Business Source Premier database. http://search.ebscohost.com/login.aspx?direct=true&db=bth&AN=13576670&site=ehost-live

Gowland, D., & Aiken, M. (2005, September). Changes to financial management performance measures, accountability factors and accounting information systems of privatized companies in Australia. *Australian Journal of Public Administration, 64*(3), 88-99. Retrieved July 25, 2007, from Business Source Premier database. http://search.ebscohost.com/login.aspx?direct=true&db=bth&AN=18102619&site=ehost-live

Essay by Marie Gould

Marie Gould is an Associate Professor and the Faculty Chair of the Business Administration Department at Peirce College in Philadelphia, Pennsylvania. She teaches in the areas of management, entrepreneurship, and international business. Although Ms. Gould has spent her career in both academia and corporate, she enjoys helping people learn new things — whether it's by teaching, developing or mentoring.

Managerial Finance

Table of Contents

Abstract
Overview
    Financial Analysis
    Efficiency
    Time Value of Money
    Capital Budgeting
    Capital Structure
    Dividends
    Cash Flow Analysis
    Financial Markets
    The Role & Decisions of the Financial Manager
    Financial Instruments
    Debt
Viewpoint
    Comparing Options for Investment & Raising Capital
    Choosing a Financial Instrument
    International Markets
    Financial Markets
    Preliminary Actions
    The Cost of Money
    Internal Managerial Finance Activities
Terms & Concepts
Bibliography
Suggested Reading

Abstract

Managing the finances of a corporation can be complex and involved and requires capable and experienced financial leadership and management. Corporations seek to provide a return on investment to stockholders and need money to finance daily operations and long term plans. Managerial finance is made up of the investment decisions financial managers make. These can be decisions about dividend policy, capital spending, funding of long and short term projects and managing long and short term debt. Financial managers also have to balance their decisions with the risk involved. Financial managers use specific tools and techniques to make investment decisions and evaluate and assess the appropriate techniques based on company strategy and current economic conditions.

Overview

Finance looks at how businesses make, use and deploy financial resources. Managerial finance considers the challenges of the financial manager who must make decisions about the techniques used to manage company finances. The decisions that the financial manager makes affect the ability of the company to adequately use its cash and liquid assets, raise funds when needed and make investment moves that benefit stockholders.

Faulkender & Wang (2006, p 1957) note that investors and shareholders care about the amount of cash that a firm has because "corporate liquidity enables firms to make investments without having to access external capital markets." In this way, companies avoid transaction costs. Companies have an objective to produce a positive financial result to ensure the continuation of the company and to provide value to investors and stockholders. When a company is publicly owned, it is important that companies make decisions that are not simply in the interest of internal stakeholders but that consider the objectives of external stakeholders such as stockholders and financial analysts. These external stakeholders are interested in predicting the profitability of a company for investment reasons.

Financial Analysis

There are two techniques of financial analysis involved in security selection and valuation. These include fundamental analysis and technical analysis.

- Fundamental analysis involves researching industry information, financial statements and other factors to determine the true value of a firm.
- Technical analysis is tracking trends and patterns that might exist in stock price.

In order to make corporate investment decisions, financial managers must understand the time value of money, capital budgeting, capital structure and dividend policy. In addition, financial managers face the problem of dealing with and making decisions about risk and return. Risk is the chance that you will get a result other than the one you expected. Other topics financial managers consider include capital budgeting, raising capital, cash flow techniques, market efficiency and the capital asset pricing model (CAPM). One technique used by financial managers is that of discounted cash flow (DCF). French (2013) provides an overview of how the DCF model is used quarterly. This technique makes sure that companies examine the income produced by capital investments.

Efficiency

Market efficiency can refer to economic efficiency or information efficiency.

- Economic efficiency has to do with how funds are allocated or directed and what the transaction cost is for these positions.
- Information efficiency refers to the availability of critical information related to investments and transactions.

Besley & Brigham (2001) note three types of information efficiency: Weak, semi-strong, and strong. Each refers to the relative strength of information related to price, price movement and how useful that information is in relation to the return on investment. The capital asset price model (CAPM) relates risk to return when considering the value of a stock. Morgenson & Harvey (2002) noted that CAPM is a model for the pricing of risky securities.

Time Value of Money

The time value of money is a statement of how one feels about money. It is the notion that a dollar today is worth more than the promise of a dollar in the future. Financial managers must observe how money reacts over time in order to decide the best use of money and what investments make sense. If a company has money tied up in investments, there is a cost that the company incurs because that money is not available to do something else. There are certain benefits of capitalizing on time. "Equity market timing" is "issuing shares at high prices and repurchasing at low prices" (Baker & Wurgler, 2002).

Capital Budgeting

Capital budgeting is the process of analyzing various investment alternatives in machinery and equipment and is used for planning long term acquisitions of capital assets. Although capital equipment may be useful for a company, the cost has to be balanced against the reward. For example, a manufacturing company may be in a position where old equipment is costing the company money because of high repair and maintenance costs and lost production. In addition, the older equipment might present a safety cost to employees and maintenance workers and may interfere with worker productivity because employees spend a lot of time dealing with equipment breakdowns. Similarly, a company may decide to invest in new equipment but it may be costly, there may be long lead times on the equipment and it may take a long time to get a return on the capital investment. Ghahremani, Aghaie, and Abedzadeh (2012) studied the effectiveness of various capital budgeting techniques over four decades and argue for the importance of adopting the real option approach to capital budgeting decisions.

Capital Structure

Capital structure refers to the framework a company uses to generate financing for assets. Companies may choose to use debt or equity financing or some combination of the two. When raising capital, a financial manager has many options. Companies can use internal money for projects or can turn to venture capital firms or banks. Loans can be obtained either as short term, working capital loans or long term loans.

Dividends

A dividend is money that is paid out of a company's profit to holders of stock. Dividend policy describes how a company will decide whether or not to pay dividends. Dividends are typically paid quarterly and can be paid out in cash or more stock to the stockholders. One of the measures of dividend policy used by financial managers is dividend yield. Dividend yield is a function of the annual dividend per share divided by the price per share (Morgenson & Harvey, 2002).

Cash Flow Analysis

An analysis of cash flow examines the in and outflows of cash and whether or not enough cash is available to meet company needs. Companies can breakeven, have a positive cash flow or net loss of cash. Projecting cash flow can prevent uncomfortable shortfalls which may result in borrowing or otherwise changing the company's financial position. However, excessive cash can uncover other signs of mismanagement. Financial managers may make changes in product prices or analyze where costs are coming from to identify the business units that generate the most in cost. Some companies find cash relief by improving their ability to collect on bills. That is why some companies employ collections agencies as an adjunct to their own accounts receivable personnel to collect stubborn, delinquent accounts. Other companies may look for ways to increase sales to bring in more cash. Financial managers also find ways to create cash reserve to prevent restrictions on company activities due to lack of cash flow.

Financial Markets

The financial markets in which the marketplace invests, buys and sells fall into the categories of markets for goods and services, financial assets, money balances, and resources (Schenk, 1997). The financial manager may deal with external parties in the course of investing or seeking financing. These institutions include banks, insurance companies and investment brokerages.

The Role & Decisions of the Financial Manager

Financial managers are responsible for acquiring needed funds for the company and positioning these funds so that they will be invested in projects that will maximize the return on investment and the enhance the value of the company.

It may sound as if the job of a managerial finance professional is an easy one and that each professional only needs to know a few formulas. However, the job is quite complex; the professional has to consider the industry, economic conditions, internal size and structure as well as financial opportunities. Pagano and Stout (2004) looked at the weighted average of cost of capital for two large firms, Microsoft and General Electric. The authors found that using three different methods, they yielded three different results, meaning that financial managers must go beyond the equations and use a myriad of techniques, subjective and objective, to make corporate investment decisions. So while financial expertise is needed and required, other skills such as decision making and weighing alternatives are also important. The financial information possessed by the financial manager must be augmented with up to date market and industry information and with new tools for analyzing corporate investments.

Managerial finance has gone through a number of evolutions regarding its context (Besley & Brigham, 2001). During the 1940s and 50s, an emphasis was placed on liquidity while the 1950s and 60s saw a shift towards maximizing the value and analysis of alternatives. Risk management was the focus of the 1970s while the 1990s considered globalization, government regulations and increased use of technology. The focus of financial managers again evolved in the post 2007 recession economy (West, 2013). Financial managers are seen as the coordinators and directors of financial decisions and must receive coherent input from other parts of the business such as operations and marketing to adequately make decisions.

Some of the ways in which financial managers optimize a company's value is by efficient forecasting and planning, coordinating major investment and financing decisions, control of financial information gathering and reporting and participating in financial markets (Besley & Brigham, 2001).

Financial Instruments

Tangible and financial assets are the primary instruments that financial managers deal with and have to maximize. A tangible asset may have value to others and can be sold or borrowed against. Similarly, financial assets are financial instruments which promise the holder a cash flow distribution at some point in the future. The types of financial instruments that financial managers may work with include equity and debt instruments such as:

- Certificates of Deposit
- Treasury Bills
- Eurodollars
- Commercial Paper
- Common Stock
- Preferred Stock
- Corporate Bonds
- Term Loans
- Treasury notes and bonds.

One of the ways in which a corporation can use financial instruments it has issued is to buy tangible assets that are income-producing assets.

Debt

Financial managers must analyze corporate activities related to short and long-term debt. Debt is when a loan is made to someone or some entity and has the features of principal value, face value, maturity value and par value. Principal value is also called principal amount or simply principle. It is equivalent to the amount being borrowed. Par, maturity or face value is the amount that will be paid on a financial security such as a bond when mature. A feature of debt that financial managers must consider is the fact that interest payments will be due in addition to principal payments. Certain types of debt result in turning over controlling interests in the company.

Some examples of short term debt are treasury bills, repurchase agreements, commercial paper and certificates of deposit. Examples of long-term debt include term loans, bonds (government treasury or municipal bonds, corporate bonds, mortgage bonds). Equity financing can take on the form of preferred or common stock. Preferred stock is preferred over common stock when dividends are distributed. Some of the features of preferred stock that are different from common stock are the possible allowance for cumulative dividends or the conversion of preferred stock into common stock (Besley & Brigham, 2001).

Common stock allows stockholders to have a stake of ownership in a firm. These stockholders may also have a preemptive right to purchase additional shares sold by the company. Capital stock is a term that refers to all the stock issued by a company and includes common and preferred stock. A company's charter authorizes the number and value of shares of stock available (Morgenson & Harvey, 2002)

Financial managers may decide to participate in the financial markets through the use of derivatives. Derivatives are financial securities based on an underlying asset like a stock or bond. Derivatives are considered to be risky investments but have the potential for a high rate of return and can possibly balance out a portfolio.

Viewpoint

Comparing Options for Investment & Raising Capital

Financial managers have many choices for investing a firm's money and must weigh those options in a way that maximizes value for the company. First, financial managers have to consider risk when choosing a financial security. One of the issues that may be important to a company is what tax implications will result from a particular type of security. In addition, the value and cost of an investment over time can impact whether or not the investment is selected for short or long term.

Choosing a Financial Instrument

The financial instrument that is best depends on your point of view. Financial managers will have to discover whether or not an investment is worthwhile from the issuer's or the investor's point of view (Besley & Brigham, 2001). Some characteristics of bonds include fixed interest payments and an interest expense that is deductible. However, they do not provide ownership and there may be some restrictions on dividends. Preferred stock may have disadvantages tax-wise by providing for higher after-tax costs because its dividends are not deductible. An advantage of preferred stock is the guarantee of a fixed payment though payouts on these fixed payments are not guaranteed. Common stock also doesn't have an obligation for companies to pay dividends but stockholders may have voting rights and some control.

International Markets

International markets offer opportunity for investment as global financial investing increases and as returns on global securities grow. Some examples of global investing include American depository receipts (ADRs) which are stocks in foreign countries where the stock is held in trust by that country's banks. There are foreign debt instruments and Eurodebt (Eurobonds, eurocredits, euro-commercial paper) available for investing. Foreign equity products include eurostock or stock that is traded in other countries or Yankee stock which is stock issued for foreign companies and traded in the U.S. (Besley & Brigham, 2001).

Financial Markets

Financial markets are the network and system of institutions, individuals, financial instruments, policies and procedures that allow borrowers and investors to get together. Financial flow can occur when a company sells its stock directly to the purchaser or when there is indirect transfer of funds through banks or intermediaries. Financial managers can choose from money markets or capital markets when investing. Money markets are for financial instruments that are typically mature within one year or less. Capital markets are markets with instruments that have maturities of greater than one year.

Preliminary Actions

There are many decisions to make when trying to raise capital for a company. Financial managers have to initially decide on the optimal amount of money needed. The type of securities required to raise the level of capital needed must also be considered. Investment bankers must be consulted to assist in navigating the market. Before setting the offer price of securities, the costs related to the offer must be itemized. A rather complex selling process involves registration with the Securities and Exchange Commission and preparing a prospectus for investors. Banks agree to underwrite the newly issued securities. The company's investment banker assists in setting up a secondary market for the securities. The Securities and Exchange Commission (SEC) is a governmental agency that regulates any issuing or trading of stocks and bonds. The SEC wants to make sure companies are not committing fraud and that investors are being given an accurate picture of what they are investing in and how. The reason for this close regulation is to prevent insider trading and manipulation of the market.

The Cost of Money

Financial managers always have to consider the cost of money. This can include interest rates on loans as well as equity to stockholders in terms of dividends and capital gains. When analyzing an opportunity, financial managers consider cost and whether or not the cost is reasonable based on what the company is allowed to invest in with money. Money can also be affected by the risk of investing in a depreciating asset that quickly loses value or inflation which makes things worth less over time. There are several categories of risk associated with cost of money decisions. These include the default risk premium which is the difference between interest rates on corporate bonds and U.S. treasury bonds. Inflation and liquidity premiums are premiums or add-ons to securities based on inflation or for securities that are not able to be made into liquid assets quickly. Interest rate risk affects investors with possible loss if the interest rates are fluctuating. Financial managers have to stay abreast of current financial information and cannot make decisions simply based on company strategy or company policy. External financial pressures can be exerted by Federal Reserve policy, changes in industries, the federal deficit or a dramatic change in business activity in the marketplace (Besley & Brigham, 2001).

Internal Managerial Finance Activities

While financial managers are well served to monitor financial news and updates, there are many activities that are central to managerial finance that take place within the confines of a company. Managerial finance often means the analysis of financial reports. Some of the reports issued by firms are consumed externally. These include the annual report which includes the basic financial statements such as the income statement, balance sheet, statement of retained earnings, cash flow statements and notes.

- An income statement is a summary of the revenues brought into the company and the expenses that were incurred by the company over the quarter or year.
- Balance sheets show the company's financial position as a snapshot of a period in time.
- The statement of cash flows shows the impact of the firm's activities such as operational cash flows, flows related to investing or financing over a certain period of time.

Knowing how much cash a company has is only part of the picture. It is important to see how the cash is used as well. Financial managers may perform ratio analysis to understand the company's liquidity position and may show how well a company manages its assets. Financial managers use ratio analysis to analyze how debt is being used and how much financing activity is taking place. Ratio analysis can also tell how profitable a company is and what the earnings are in relation to other companies in similar industries or of similar size. Although ratio analysis provides a lot of information, it can be misleading if the company has several different business units that operate in different or multiple industries. It can be complex to extract an accurate picture and extrapolate that to financial decision making.

Finally, financial managers are responsible for financial planning and control. The planning aspect involves projecting the sales and income based on the company's sales efforts and current production levels. In addition, financial managers must determine the resources needed to implement financial plans. Control is monitoring that takes place to make sure the companies activities are in line with plans and to make adjustments where needed. Monitoring and planning are assisted by automation and are ongoing processes that are subject to change based on internal or external forces.

Terms & Concepts

Abandonment Option: When the choice is made to abandon an investment instead of waiting for the investment to produce a return.

Bankruptcy Risk: Sometimes called insolvency risk. The risk for companies associated with having liabilities that exceed assets. Also called negative net worth.

Debt: A relationship where a borrower receives funds from a lender and is obligated to pay back the lending amount plus interest.

Debt Financing: Raising capital by selling debt financial instruments such as notes, bills and bonds to individuals or institutions.

Equity: Ownership in a company.

Equity Financing: Raising capital by selling shares of stock.

Net Present Value: The current value of cash flow in the future minus cost.

Pecking-order: Preferred order of financing options.

Present Value: The value of a dollar today that is equal to the value of a dollar in the future.

Bibliography

Baker, M. & Wurgler, J. (2002). Market timing and capital structure. *Journal of Finance, 57*(1), 1. Retrieved October 1, 2007, from EBSCO Online Database Business Source Complete. http://search.ebscohost.com/login.aspx?direct=true&db=bth&AN=5889290&site=ehost-live

Besley, S. & Brigham, E.F. (2001). *Principles of finance* (2nd ed.). Boston: Southwest College Publishing.

Faulkender, M. & Wang, R. (2006). Corporate financial policy and the value of cash. *Journal of Finance, 61*(4), 1957-1990. Retrieved October 1, 2007, from EBSCO Online Database Business Source Complete. http://search.ebscohost.com/login.aspx?direct=true&db=bth&AN=21796398&site=ehost-live

French, N. (2013). The discounted cash flow model for property valuations: Quarterly cash flows. *Journal of Property Investment & Finance, 31*(2), 208-212. Retrieved on November 15, 2013, from EBSCO Online Database Business Source Complete. http://search.ebscohost.com/login.aspx?direct=true&db=bth&AN=85804861&site=ehost-live

Ghahremani, M., Aghaie, A., & Abedzadeh, M. (2012). Capital budgeting technique selection through four decades: With a great focus on real option. *International Journal of Business & Management, 7*(17), 98-119. Retrieved on November 15, 2013, from EBSCO Online Database Business Source Complete. http://search.ebscohost.com/login.aspx?direct=true&db=bth&AN=80037203&site=ehost-live

Gordon, R. & Lee, Y. (2007) Interest rates, taxes and corporate financial policies. *National Tax Journal, 60*(1), 65-84. Retrieved October 1, 2007, from EBSCO Online Database Business Source Complete. http://search.ebscohost.com/

login.aspx?direct=true&db=bth&AN=24699957&site=ehost-live

Morgenson, G. & Harvey, C. R. (2002). *The New York Times Dictionary of Money Investing*. New York: Times Books.

Pagano, M.S. & Stout, D.E. (2004). Calculating a firm's cost of capital. *Management Accounting Quarterly, 12*(3), 243 — 256. Retrieved November 18, 2007, from EBSCO Online Database Business Source Complete. http://search.ebscohost.com/login.aspx?direct=true&db=buh&AN=14027648&site=ehost-live

Schenk, R. (1997). *Overview: financial markets*. Retrieved November 21, 2007 from http://ingrimayne.com/econ/Financial/Overview8ma.html.

West, P. (2013). Thriving in the post-crisis economy: Managing a nexus of capabilities. *Strategic Direction, 29*(4), 3-6. Retrieved on November 15, 2013, from EBSCO Online Database Business Source Complete. http://search.ebscohost.com/login.aspx?direct=true&db=bth&AN=86655297&site=ehost-live

Suggested Reading

Czurak, D. (2007). City getting a bond aid. *Grand Rapids Business Journal, 25*(44), 3-7. Retrieved November 18, 2007, from EBSCO Online Database Business Source Complete. http://search.ebscohost.com/login.aspx?direct=true&db=buh&AN=27261837&site=ehost-live

Krishnan, C. N. V. (2007). Optimal wage contracts under asymmetric information and moral hazard when investment decisions are delegated. *Journal of Economics & Finance, 31*(3), 302-318. Retrieved November 18, 2007, from EBSCO Online Database Business Source Complete. http://search.ebscohost.com/login.aspx?direct=true&db=buh&AN=27439574&site=ehost-live

Mankin, E. (2007). Measuring innovation performance. *Research Technology Management, 50*(6), 5-7. Retrieved November 18, 2007, from EBSCO Online Database Business Source Complete. http://search.ebscohost.com/login.aspx?direct=true&db=buh&AN=27377099&site=ehost-live

Schoder, D. (2007). The flaw in customer lifetime value. *Harvard Business Review, 85*(12), 26. Retrieved November 18, 2007, from EBSCO Online Database Business Source Complete. http://search.ebscohost.com/login.aspx?direct=true&db=buh&AN=27329791&site=ehost-live

Essay by Marlanda English, Ph. D.

Dr. Marlanda English is president of ECS Consulting Associates which provides executive coaching and management consulting services. ECS also provides online professional development content. Dr. English was previously employed in various engineering, marketing and management positions with IBM, American Airlines, Borg-Warner Automotive and Johnson & Johnson. Dr. English holds a doctorate in business with a major in organization and management and a specialization in e-business.

Strategic Financial Management

Table of Contents

Abstract

Overview
- Reviewing the Past:
- Forecasting the Future:
- Setting Strategies & Plans:
- Set Annual Budgets:

Application
- Financial Policies
- Finances & Daily Activities
- Creating a Successful Financial Plan

Viewpoint
- Statistical Sampling

Conclusion

Terms & Concepts

Bibliography

Suggested Reading

Abstract

This article focuses on how organizations such as nonprofits may create a financial system that allows them to manage their operations and maintain financial stability. The article provides recommendations on how to create and implement policies that will support a strong financial system as well as a process that auditors may use in order to audit the records.

Overview

In order for organization's to be successful, they must create a strategic plan that will position the firm for growth and competitiveness. The senior management team will need to analyze all data, including the financial records, to ensure that the organization can make a profit, remain competitive and be positioned for continued growth.

A social service organization (Making Ends Meet, n.d.) identified four important stages in the financial planning process. These stages are reviewing the past, forecasting the future, setting strategies and plans, and setting annual budgets. Each of these phases is of equal importance and some of the tasks at each phase include:

Reviewing the Past:
- Monitor recent trends in demand and expenditure
- Monitor trends in funding streams
- Monitor and report on actual performance and outcomes, including end-of-year position and performance against specific performance indicators for similar organizations
- Collect comparative information about actual costs and cost drivers
- Review the results and evaluate the recommendations from any external inspection reports and management letters from external auditors (Strategic financial planning, n.d., "Stages of financial planning").

Forecasting the Future:
- Evaluate the impact of national policies and strategies
- Identify and estimate levels of the various funding streams
- Review the impact of local policy initiatives and priorities
- Determine the future impact of known trends on demand and expenditure
- Identify the financial implications of demographic trends and other "drivers" of demand which are outside the control of the organization (Strategic financial planning, n.d., "Stages of financial planning").

Setting Strategies & Plans:
- Take into account the corporate context for strategic planning
- Link financial planning with service, human resource and asset management planning

- Collect information on the knowledge and skill base required for effective budget management at all organizational levels
- Engage all key stakeholders in the strategic financial planning (Strategic financial planning, n.d., "Stages of financial planning").

Set Annual Budgets:
- Come to consensus on what the budget process should be
- Ensure budgets are informed by financial plans
- Involve budget managers in budget setting
- Match commitments and expected changes in demand with resources available
- Respond to unexpected changes
- Review budget structures
- Engage with key stakeholders
- Ensure short term decisions in budget setting do not undermine longer-term priorities and strategies.

As the organization goes through the financial planning process, key decision makers should determine the types of policies that need to be in effect in order to be successful at each of the individual phases.

Application

Financial Policies

The board of directors is very important in the governance of non-profit — 501(c)(3) organizations. Individuals who accept these positions are committed to organizational oversight. Part of this responsibility includes making sure that the organization is fiscally sound. Loyalty, care and obedience are considered to be three basic functions of trustees and these three functions are the benchmark for financial policies created by the board of directors (National Center for Nonprofit Boards, 1996).

What does each of these functions symbolize?

- Loyalty implies that the board members will act in the best interest of the organization and avoid any actions or decisions that will appear to be a conflict of interest with the mission of the organization.
- Care refers to the promise that board members will review, critique, and respond to any reports that are related to the organization, especially as it relates to management, programs and financial matters.
- Obedience ensures that the organization will adhere to all laws and regulations that affect the operation of the organization.

In order to successfully fulfill these obligations, the board of directors should ensure that they are able to:

- Make decisions that are in the best interest of the organization;
- Enforce guidelines that prohibit the use of assets to benefit professional staff or the board members;
- Assist in preventing conflicts of interest;
- Make sure there is a quorum at each meeting so that important decisions can be made; especially at meetings that will allow the organization to operate smoothly (National Center for Nonprofit Boards, 1996, p. 5).

Finances & Daily Activities

One of the most important decisions that a board can make concerns the daily operation of the organization. The board should have a clear understanding of the organization's financial status. Financial decisions and transactions are critical to the daily activities of the organization. Therefore, it is imperative that there are policies in place that will assist the staff members with performing daily activities. In order to achieve financial stability, the board must develop and implement a "system of financial accountability, a financial plan that reflects the organization's mission, a sound investment strategy, and adequate reserves" (National Center for Nonprofit Boards, 1996, p. 6).

Creating a Successful Financial Plan

Once the board has an understanding of the organization's financial position, it can create strategic policies to manage the organization's financial structure. The National Center for Nonprofit Boards (1996) recommended a five step process to creating a successful financial plan for 501(c)(3) organizations.

- **Step 1 — Establish the Structure** Since the magnitude of work would be too much for a single person, the responsibilities of an effective financial planning and oversight should be divided among all of the board members. The professional staff and other resources should be used as necessary. Although the full board is ultimately held responsible for decision making, there are laws that support delegating the task of financial evaluation and assessment to committees. When establishing the financial structure, the board is responsible for:
- Making sure that the responsibilities for financial oversight are covered through the committee structure;
- Scrutinizing all financial considerations before they come to the floor for board vote; and
- Overseeing everything that the board does.
- **Step 2 — Define Responsibilities and Set Limits** The designation and clarification of financial responsibilities and limits are necessary so that an organization can avoid confusion and minimize conflict. By adhering to this rule,

an organization should be able to successfully complete and submit Form 990 to the Internal Revenue Service. When the board defines responsibilities and sets limits, it should:

- Make clear assignments of financial responsibility;

- Be responsible for carefully reviewing financial reports submitted to governmental agencies, such as the Internal Revenue Service, to ensure that there are no problems; and

- Create guidelines that prohibit expenditures for certain purposes and outline limits in other areas. This information should be detailed in financial policy statements.

- **Step 3 — Understand and Use Available Tools** Since most board members are not seasoned financial experts, it is important for each board member to have access to the tools that will assist them with understanding the financial ramifications of an organization's actions. As a result, the board should:

- Structure financial policies that compliment and strengthen the strategic plan;

- Use the budget as a tool for setting financial policy;

- Review the organization's revenue sources to determine whether they are sustainable;

- Build and monitor the organization's reserve funds to safeguard against unexpected events;

- Use financial statements to evaluate whether actual expenditures match the goals of the budget and strategic plan; and

- Write a policy specifying acceptable uses for reserve funds; and

- Use the audit to check internal systems, and carefully review the audit before accepting it.

- **Step 4 — Use Internal Resources Strategically** When creating financial policies, the board should identify and appoint the key players as well as monitor the authority that is given to each person. Three of the key players tend to be the chief executive; the staff finance officer; and the treasurer. Board members are responsible for:

- Appointing and monitoring the chief executive and key staff;

- Ensuring that the staff members receive adequate training to upgrade their skills;

- Regulating the power given to each individual who has financial responsibilities;

- Implementing a policy that requires two signature authorizations for checks that exceed a predetermined amount;

- Regulating the chief executive's capability of accepting gifts or committing to investments without first gaining board authorization;

- Creating a "check and balance" with functions in order to prevent fraudulent activities; and

- Investigating how to get bonding insurance for the treasurer and key staff.

- **Step 5 — Effectively Use External Resources** The board may need the assistance of external resources, such as consultants, in order to operate efficiently. The board should:

- Choose a bank that is federally insured and not connected to the organization;

- Review insurance policies to determine if the organization provides adequate coverage;

- Develop an investment policy that clearly conveys the board's investment goals and their link to the organization's mission;

- Avoid unnecessary investment risks;

- Ensure that investments are structured to allow for immediate availability of cash; and

- Hire a qualified investment consultant and monitor results on a regular basis.

Viewpoint

Statistical Sampling

The previous section described how 501(c)(3) organizations can set up their financial system in order to monitor key personnel and the processes that they have in place. A five step process was presented, and the third step indicated that there should be an audit to check internal systems. An organization may suggest that an internal or external auditor check their books. Auditors are continually seeking new tools to assist with the auditing function so that they do not have to rely on their judgment. "To meet their clients' needs in environment of heightened competition and runaway inflation, many auditors are turning to scientifically supported methods of planning, executing and evaluating audit procedures to obtain evidential matter. Statistical sampling is one such method" (Akresh & Zuber, 1981, p. 50). There are many ways that an accountant can set up a statistical sampling. Hitzig (2004) provided a model that worked on the premise that one could set up a statistical sampling by defining the population, frame and sampling unit.

- **The Population** The population is the combination of every account or transaction that the auditor desires to use in order to arrive at the conclusion. The first step in the process is to define the test objective. Once the test objective has been determined, the auditor should define the population. The steps are in this order so that the auditor can draw a sample based on the specific test objective.

- **The Frame** Once the testing has been completed, the auditor must attribute the results to the items versus the population since auditors tend not to choose a sample straight from the population itself. This representation is referred to as the frame. The frame allows the auditor to establish a foundation for further identification of items that should be incorporated into a sample.

In most cases, the accounting population is presented in a list format (i.e. payroll file, accounts receivable detail). This list (or frame) tends to streamline and simplify the sample selection process. However, the population's sample frame is not required to be a list. Sometimes, the geographical locations that floor plans or other population identifiers can reveal are used as frames. Also, there may be an occasion where the auditor has to create an appropriate frame when one is not available. Regardless of whether or not a list is used, the selection of a frame is usually centered on availability and usefulness. The frames that prove to be the most accessible are computer data files. If these files are used, there is an opportunity to integrate them by applying computer-assisted auditing methods and data retrieval techniques.

There are some circumstances where the auditor has to be on alert to make sure that they do not encounter any problems with their samplings. Hitzig (2004) provided some examples such as:

- Over Specified Frames

In the event that there are frame units that fail to include population membership, the units are not applied to the end result that the auditor might be looking for.

- Underspecified or Incomplete Frames

As the auditor makes plans to collect a sample, he/she must ensure that each item seen in the population is simultaneously included in the frame. If the frame is not completed, then there is a probability of some significant members of the population not being accounted for in the sample. If this type of action were to occur, "there is a violation of AU 350's requirement for representativeness, which requires that every item in the population under examination must have a chance of being selected. If a frame is incomplete, there is an opportunity for biased estimates of the population value that is under examination. This statement is true especially if the auditor is not careful to distinguish between the size of the population and the size of the frame on which the selection of the sample was performed" (Hitzig, 2004, "Overspecified Frames").

- **The Sampling Unit** A population is comprised of basic units that are assembled to form the sampling unit. The sampling unit is determined by the auditor's choice of frame. The item that the auditor conducts the examination upon is referred to as the sampling unit, and the sampling unit is vouched or traced. The examination can be conducted by inspection, observation or confirmation.

Auditors tend to make the statistical sampling procedures flexible. If the collection and assessment processes are performed adequately, there is a high probability that there will not be any questions regarding validity due to technical issues. For example, if the total documented amount of the sampling units is equivalent to the total documented amount of the population being scrutinized, then the technical information is validated and accepted. Therefore, it is considered genuine.

How are sampling units selected? Auditors have different preferences. However, listed below are some common trends in the field.

- **Accounts.** Accounts are the preferred method of sampling unit, especially if dealing with consumer accounts (i.e. credit cards). Using this approach will allow the auditor to precisely confirm the net balance in any designated account. However, there may be problems if an auditor attempts to confirm account balances on commercial accounts. Therefore, commercial accounts tend to be controlled through vouchers payable systems.

- **Open invoices.** If an organization has a collection of open invoices that are ready to be accessed right away, then open invoices would be the preferred method. Since the open invoices only consist of debits to the accounts receivable, the auditor will need to administer a different test technique for crediting the accounts.

Since many organizations document their purchases in a vouchers payable method, they have found that it is simpler to validate separate invoices versus account balances. This selection of sampling units can also be associated with equal probability (i.e. basic random sampling) or with probability in relation to size (i.e. dollar-unit sampling).

- **Invoice line items.** Dollar-unit sampling allows an auditor to select a particular invoice line product as the indicated sampling unit. Such an approach is referred to as subsampling (Leslie, Teitlebaum, & Anderson, 1980). In this scenario, "a computer program identifies the invoice and the dollar within the invoice in which the selected line item is located. The auditor is responsible for manually identifying the line item by footing the invoice until the selected item is found. The auditor only has to vouch for that item, and every other selected line item in the sample. In dollar-unit sampling, the auditor projects the results associated with the selected line items by using the total book value of the frame as the representation of the frame size" (Hitzig, 2004, "Invoice line items").

Conclusion

In order for organization's to be successful, they must create a strategic plan that will position the firm for growth and competitiveness. The senior management team will need to analyze all data, including the financial records, to ensure that the organization can make a profit, remain competitive and be positioned for continued growth. As the organization goes through the process, key decision makers should determine the types of policies that need to be in effect in order to be successful at each of the individual phases.

The board of directors is very important in the governance of non-profit — 501(c)(3) organizations. Individuals who accept these positions are committed to organizational oversight. Part of this responsibility includes making sure that the organization is fiscally sound. Loyalty, care and obedience are considered to be three basic functions of trustees and these three functions are the benchmark for financial policies created by the board of directors (National Center for Nonprofit Boards, 1996).

An organization may suggest that an internal or external auditor check their books. Auditors are continually seeking new tools to assist with the auditing function so that they do not have to rely on their judgment. "To meet their clients' needs in environment of heightened competition and runaway inflation, many auditors are turning to scientifically supported methods of planning, executing and evaluating audit procedures to obtain evidential matter. Statistical sampling is one such method" (Akresh & Zuber, 1981, p. 50). There are many ways that an accountant can set up a statistical sampling.

Terms & Concepts

501(c)(3): The section of the Internal Revenue Code that grants tax exemption to nonprofit institutions such as religious, educational, charitable, and scientific organizations.

Audit: A formal assessment of an organization's accounting records. Audits are traditionally performed by independent public accounting firms.

Board of Directors: Qualified individuals who are chosen by a company's shareholders to supervise and manage the company.

Dollar Unit Sampling: A method that incorporates a combined-attributes-and-variables method of inferring through the use of statistics. The technique is useful in sampling variables and attributes at the same time, but it is unique due to its establishment of sampling units as separate and solitary dollars instead of physical units like inventory items. The dollar unit sampling methods are usually carried out on the inventory items that contain the dollars chosen.

Financial Statements: Reports prepared at the end of an accounting period that include statements of economic standing, statements of activity, and statements of cash flow status.

Frame: When the auditor attributes the results of a testing to the items versus the population, he or she will come up with a list. This list allows that the auditor have a strong foundation with which to identify items that will then be part of a larger sample.

Population: The assortment of all files and accounts that the auditor wants to use in order to arrive at the conclusion.

Reserves: Resources accumulated above the amount necessary to cover operating expenses.

Sampling Unit: A unit that an aggregate is divided into in order for further sampling to commence. Each individual unit is selected separately, distinctively, and indivisibly.

Statistical Sampling: A technique of choosing a part of a population through calculating the mathematical probabilities involved. Such sampling helps to make more sound and scientific inferences having to do with the traits of the whole population.

Bibliography

Akresh, A., & Zuber, G. (1981). Exploring statistical sampling. *Journal of Accountancy, 151*(2), 50-56. Retrieved August 25, 2007, from EBSCO Online Database Business Source Complete. http://search.ebscohost.com/login.aspx?direct=true&db=bth&AN=4585670&site=ehost-live

Bryce, H. (1996). *The nonprofit board's role in establishing financial policies.* Washington, DC: National Center for Nonprofit Boards.

Hitzig, N. (2004). Elements of sampling: The population, the frame, and the sampling unit. *CPA Journal, 74*(11), 30-33. Retrieved August 26, 2007, from EBSCO Online Database Business Source Complete. http://search.ebscohost.com/login.aspx?direct=true&db=bth&AN=15023175&site=ehost-live

Leslie, D., Teitlebaum, A., & Anderson, R. (1980). *Dollar unit sampling: A practical guide for auditors.* London: Pitman.

Mf Saltaji, I. (2013). Corporate governance relationship with strategic management. *Internal Auditing & Risk Management, 8*(2), 293-300. Retrieved November 15, 2013, from EBSCO Online Database Business Source Complete. http://search.ebscohost.com/login.aspx?direct=true&db=bth&AN=90542685&site=ehost-live

Robertson, C., Blevins, D., & Duffy, T. (2013). A five-year review, update, and assessment of ethics and governance in strategic management journal. *Journal of Business Ethics, 117*(1), 85-91. Retrieved November 15, 2013, from EBSCO Online Database Business Source Complete. http://search.ebscohost.com/login.aspx?direct=true&db=bth&AN=90521145&site=ehost-live

Strategic financial planning. (n.d.). *Making ends meet: A website for managing the money in social services.* Retrieved September 3, 2007, from http://www.joint-reviews.gov.uk/money/Financialmgt/1-22.html

Wang, T., & Bansal, P. (2012). Social responsibility in new ventures: profiting from a long-term orientation. *Strategic Management Journal, 33*(10), 1135-1153.Retrieved November 15, 2013, from EBSCO Online Database Business Source Complete. http://search.ebscohost.com/login.aspx?direct=true&db=bth&AN=78388200&site=ehost-live

Suggested Reading

Agundu, P. (2005). Strategic management dynamics: Training imperatives for up-moving accounting and financial professionals in the banking industry. *Finance India, 19*(2), 525-533. Retrieved August 26, 2007, from EBSCO Online Database Business Source Complete. http://search.ebscohost.com/login.aspx?direct=true&db=bth&AN=18775463&site=ehost-live

Bromiley, P., & James-Wade, S. (2003). Putting rational blinders behind us: Behavioural understandings of finance and strategic management. *Long Range Planning, 36*(1), 37-49. Retrieved August 26, 2007, from EBSCO Online Database Business Source Complete. http://search.ebscohost.com/login.aspx?direct=true&db=bth&AN=9340554&site=ehost-live

Hyperion financial management, strategic finance, reports & analyzer. (2004). *DM Review, 14*(2), 75. Retrieved August 25, 2007, from EBSCO Online Database Business Source Complete. http://search.ebscohost.com/login.aspx?direct=true&db=bth&AN=12432153&site=ehost-live

Essay by Marie Gould

Marie Gould is an Associate Professor and the Faculty Chair of the Business Administration Department at Peirce College in Philadelphia, Pennsylvania. She teaches in the areas of management, entrepreneurship, and international business. Although Ms. Gould has spent her career in both academia and corporate, she enjoys helping people learn new things — whether it's by teaching, developing or mentoring.

Financing the Corporation

Table of Contents

Abstract

Overview
- Two Options of Financing
- Debt Financing
- Commercial Banks
- Debt Financing: To Diversify or Not?
- Equity Capital
- Venture Capitalists
- Angel Investors

Application
- Types of Corporate Venturing

Viewpoint
- Funding
- Trends in Financing

Conclusion

Terms & Concepts

Bibliography

Suggested Reading

Abstract

This article focuses on how to finance a corporation. One of the greatest challenges for new ventures is the ability to secure capital that will allow the corporation to grow. There is no magic formula, and the management team will need to evaluate and assess which options are beneficial for the company. Each business will need to weigh the pros and cons of each option in order to determine what would be best. There are two options that these businesses may consider. The two types of financing - debt financing and equity capital - are explored. The role of commercial banks, the Small Business Administration, angel investors, and venture capitalists is introduced and discussed.

Overview

Corporations believe in the success of their dream, and they expect their ventures to take off and expand. One of the greatest challenges for new ventures is the ability to secure capital for investments that will allow the company to grow. All projects will reach a crossroad where sufficient cash flow is necessary in order to go to the next level. It could be after a period of time or it could be because the venture was so popular and the company is growing at a rapid rate due to demand. Regardless of the situation, the company's management team will need to determine when and how they will invest in the future through, for example, purchasing new equipment, hiring new staff or putting more money into marketing initiatives. Raising money can be a difficult task if the company has not established a reputation or is still new.

When determining the amount of capital needed, the decision makers must analyze the situation and decide how much and what type of capital is required. Since the situation is not the same for all businesses, there is no magical formula. Some businesses may only need short term financing for items such as salaries and inventory; whereas, other businesses may need long term financing for major items such as office space and equipment. Each business must develop a customized plan that will meet its unique needs.

Securing capital is a choice made after weighing the pros and cons of various options. There are three popular sources for obtaining funding for new ventures: borrowing from financial institutions, partnering with venture capitalists, and selling equity and possession in order to obtain a share of the revenue (Goel & Hasan, 2004). All financing options can be classified into two categories: debt financing and equity capital.

- Debt financing may include bank loans, personal and family contributions and financing from agencies such as the Small Business Administration. Loans are often secured by some type of collateral in the company and are paid off over a period of time with interest.

- On the other hand, venture capitalists and angel investors provide funding in the form of equity capital.

Pierce (2005) offers some advice which may be of assistance when assessing which option may be best for the company. Some of the tips include:

- A Small Business Administration program may not be the best option if the company needs less than $50,000.

- Debt financing is often less expensive and easier to obtain than equity capital. Financing the venture via debt entails the responsibility of making monthly payments regardless of whether the business has an affirmative cash flow.

- Equity investors assume that there will be very little return during the beginning stages of the profession, but need additional research about the business' development. In addition, they assume that the company will definitely succeed in achieving the aforementioned aims and objectives.

- Debt financing is often offered to all forms of corporations. However, equity capital tends to be reserved for companies with quick and significant growth potential.

- Angel investors tend to invest money in companies that are within a 50-mile radius, and the amounts of funding tend to be in the range of $25,000 and $250,000. Angel investors may be companions, relatives, customers, suppliers, financial experts or even competitors.

- It is difficult to secure venture capital funding, even in a good economy.

Two Options of Financing

Debt financing and equity capital options both require the financial professionals of an organization to complete detailed documentation prior to the award of financing. The finance team should be prepared to produce quarterly balance sheets, background information on the company and projections.

Debt Financing
Commercial Banks

If the company cannot finance the expansion through personal investments, the management team will need to develop a business plan that meets the criteria for potential lenders. Commercial banks may be the first choice, especially if the owner has a relationship with a specific lender. Since traditional lenders tend to be conservative, good rapport and an established relationship will be beneficial when applying for a loan. According to the University of Maine's Cooperative Extension, a 1980 Wisconsin study of smaller corporations discovered that 25% of the companies that underwent the interview process were denied at first, but 75% of them were approved when they submitted their proposal to another group. It is important for potential borrowers to understand the mindset of potential lenders. Most lenders tend to focus on five important factors when deciding whether or not to extend credit, and business owners need to be prepared to address them. The five factors are:

- **Character** — what are your personal characteristics? Are you ethical and have a good reputation? Will you do everything possible to pay the loan back?

- **Capacity** — will your business be able to generate sufficient cash flow to pay the loan back? Do you have access to other income?

- **Collateral** — do you have collateral to cover the loan in the event the venture does not perform well? Is there a qualified individual willing to co-sign on the loan?

- **Conditions** — have you researched the environment to see if there are any circumstances that could negatively impact your business (i.e. nature of product, competition)? How will you deal with these situations if they arise?

- **Capital** — what are you personally willing to invest in the venture? Most lenders are not willing to invest in ventures if you have not made a major investment in the future of the project. Why should they invest in the venture if you are not willing or able to?

Debt Financing: To Diversify or Not?

Colla, Ippolito, and Li (2013), looking at debt structure using a newer, comprehensive database of types of debt employed by public U.S. firms, found that 85% of the sample firms borrow "predominantly with one type of debt, and the degree of debt specialization varies widely across different subsamples." Large, rated firms tend to diversify across multiple debt types, while small, unrated firms specialize in fewer types. The authors showed that firms employing few types of debt "have higher bankruptcy costs, are more opaque, and lack access to some segments of the debt markets" (Colla, Ippolito, & Li, 2013).

Equity Capital
Venture Capitalists

Venture capital is usually available for start-up companies with a product or idea that may be risky, but has a high potential of yielding above average profits. Funds are invested in ventures that have not been discovered. The money may come from wealthy individuals, government sponsored Small Business Investment Corporations (SBICs), insurance companies, and corporations. It is more difficult to obtain financing from venture capitalists. A company must provide a formal proposal such as a business plan so that the venture capitalist may conduct a thorough evaluation of the company's records. Venture capitalists only approve a small percentage of the proposals that they receive, and they tend to favor innovative technical ventures.

Funding may be invested throughout the company's life cycle with funding being provided at both the beginning and later stages of growth. Venture capitalists may invest at different stages. Some firms may invest before the idea has been fully developed while others may provide funding during the early stages of the company's life. However, there is a group of venture capitalists who specialize in assisting companies when they have reached the point when the company needs financing in order to expand the business.

Angel Investors

Many firms receive some type of funding prior to seeking capital from venture capitalists. Angel Investors have been identified as one source that entrepreneurs may reach out to for assistance (Gompers, 1995). "In a nationwide survey of more than 3,000 individual angel investors conducted by the Angel Capital Association, more than 96 percent predict they'll invest in at least one new company in 2007. Also, 77 percent expect to invest in three to nine startups, and five percent think they'll fund 10 or more new companies" (Edelhauser, 2007). This is good news for entrepreneurs with a dream.

Including angel investors in the early stages of financing could improve the changes of receiving venture capital financing. Madill, Haines and Riding (2005) conducted a study with small businesses and found that "57% of the firms that had received angel investor financing had also received financing from venture capitalists. Firms that did not receive angel" investing in the early stages (approximately 10% of the firms in the study) did not obtain venture capital funding (Madill, et. al., 2005, "Abstract"). It appears that angel investor financing is a significant factor in obtaining venture capital funding. Since obtaining venture capital tends to be difficult, businesses can benefit from the contacts and experience of angel investors in order to prepare for a venture capital application and evaluation. The intervention of an angel investor may make the company appear more attractive to the venture capitalists.

Regardless of how a company decides to finance the venture, it will have to make an agreement that is beneficial to the investor since they are the ones providing the money. Therefore, it is important to select a choice that benefits the business in the long run. Initial decisions may set the tone for future deals. Advani (2006) has provided some recommendations to consider when determining what will work best. These suggestions include:

- **Don't give pro-rata rights to your first investors.** If your first investor is given pro-rata rights, chances are your future investors will want the same agreement. It would be wise to balance the needs of your early investors to protect their stake in the company with how attractive the company will be to future investors.
- **Avoid giving too many people the right to be overly involved.** If too many people are involved, it could create a bureaucracy and make it difficult for decisions to be made in a timely manner. In addition, the daily tasks of a business may be prolonged due to the need for multiple authorization signatures.
- **Beware of any limits placed on management compensation.** Some investors may place a cap on the earning potential of senior management personnel. This type of action could create a problem with human resource needs such as attracting and hiring quality talent to run and grow the business.
- **Request a cure period.** Many investors will request representation for every legal agreement to protect themselves if the management of a company is not in compliance with laws, licenses, and regulations that govern the operation of the business. Although all parties may have good intentions, errors do occur. If a "cure period" is added to the financing agreement, the entrepreneur will have the opportunity to find a solution to the problem within a given period of time (i.e. two to four weeks).
- **Restrict your share restrictions.** Having unrestricted shares is often a good negotiating factor with future investors. Therefore, it would be wise to evaluate any requests to restrict the sale of shares owned by the founders and/or management team.

Application

Types of Corporate Venturing

The first corporate venture funds appeared in the mid-1960s, which was approximately 20 years following the first formation of the institutional venture capital funds (Gompers, 2002). "Since that time, corporate venturing has undergone three boom-or-bust cycles that closely track the independent venture capital sector" (Gompers, 2002, p. 2). It has been found that many corporations will consider entering the business venture market when the independent sector starts to show hints of achievement and prosperity (Gompers & Lerner, 1998).

Large corporations have shown an interest in venture capital investing over the years, and they tend to use many different means to achieve their clever and budgeting aims for venture capital investments. Gomper (2002) described three of these models, which are internal corporate venture group, dedicated external fund, and passive limited partner in a venture. What is involved with these three models? Some organizations will create an internal corporate venture group to assess venture capital options and invest successfully. Other corporations will put investment capital in a loyal fund that exists as a separate entity external to the organization. Finally, there are real venture funds that offer businesses the chance to be acquiescent, limited partners and perform diverse investments in ambitious corporations.

Viewpoint

Funding

In order to avoid a "backlash of no cash," a business may determine that selling shares of equity would be the best way to secure working capital. This alternative could alleviate some of the stress associated with starting a new venture and provides the company an opportunity to grow at a quicker rate. However, the business will be required to give the investors some control and profits. Angel investors may want to take a role in the company, but the venture capitalists will probably want to remain in the background as a silent partner. If the venture is not successful, the investor loses. Therefore, angel investors and venture capitalists will probably require a higher return on investment than a conventional lender since the risks are greater.

Trends in Financing

New ventures will continue to grow, and corporate management teams will need to look to the trends when determining how to finance. From about 2006 to 2008, the availability of financing and the cost of options changed. Advani (2006) provided a list of trends that might assist corporations in getting funding for new ventures at the time of his writing. The trends for start-up financing in 2007 were:

- Angel investing continued to grow. "There were about 250,000 angel investors in the United States investing in approximately 50,000 small companies each year," and this number was expected to continue to grow as angel investing became more popular (Advani, 2006, ¶ 2). One reason for the growth may have been the proposed tax incentives at the time that were to be provided to high-net-worth investors who privately invest.
- Valuations and investment terms were good. "The yield rate on angel investments (the rate at which investments presented to angels result in funding) increased from 10 percent in 2003 to 23 percent in 2005. Pre-launch startup valuations involving first-time corporations escalated to more than $5 million. However, they were expected to stabilize at $2 million to $3 million in the future" (Advani, 2006, ¶ 4).
- Business credit scores supplemented personal credit scores. As of the mid-2000s, credit cards remained the most used form of capital for companies wanting to finance their debt. In the past, credit card companies made decisions based on the owner's personal credit history, but more recently many companies are using credit data on the business to make decisions. Business credit information may be collected from data banks such as the Small Business Financial Exchange (SBFE). Banks and other lenders utilize the information on the companies in conjunction with their supported instructions for businesses. Nearly every one of the top 20 banks in the United States was using this method as of about 2007.
- Getting $50,000 in funding continued to be difficult. According to the Global Corporationship Monitor, the average amount of start-up capital used by small businesses in industrialized countries was $53,000 as of the mid-2000s (Advani, 2006, ¶ 6). Unfortunately, most corporations could not secure $50,000 in credit card financing, and angel investors were usually not interested in companies where they were the only investor in businesses with insufficient working capital. In addition, programs, such as the Small Business Administration's Micro Loan Program, were facing cuts and so weren't being marketed by SBA lenders. However, nonprofit micro lenders were sometimes able to fill the gap. In the past, these lenders were not able to compete with banks, but as of the mid-2000s they were considering forming an alliance to more effectively convert credit bureau protocol to include performance of micro loans in credit scores. This action may make this option more attractive to corporations and small business owners.

In fact, Paul Quintero, CEO of microlender Accion East in New York, said in 2013 that although he lends to mom-and-pop business owners who typically do not qualify for bank loans, his hope is that banks will someday view microlending as a "viable line of business" (Kline, 2013). Accion's loan rates are attractive to potential borrowers at around 12% as of 2013, but "depository institutions, with their built-in funding advantages, could offer even lower rates, and Quintero would have no problem ceding business to them if it reduced customers' borrowing costs" (Kline, 2013).

- Low credit scores were no longer considered harmful to financing, but patient capital remained a significant obstruction to potential success. In the past, if a potential corporation did not have a high credit score, credit options were limited. Many used the equity in their homes in order to get a good rate. But Internet lenders and non-traditional one-on-one lenders have developed alternatives for businesses without high credit scores. Although the cost of the capital may be higher for those without a good credit score, options exist. Unfortunately, the lack of patient capital and long-term financing choices for companies with sub-prime credit presents problems. The interest rates that these companies charge can be very high and businesses may not be able to generate earnings while paying these rates.

As for venture-capital trends, venture capitalists invested $8.1 billion into 981 U.S.-based companies in the final quarter of 2012, according to Fortune.com and PitchBook Data (Primack, 2013). Those numbers show little change from the previous quarter and suggest that year-end 2013 totals will be a bit lower than in 2012. Furthermore, venture capitalists are "acquiring smaller and smaller stakes of portfolio companies upon investment, particularly on Series A deals. Back in 2004, VCs acquired 40% of a company on Series A rounds and 24% of a company on Series D rounds." For the first three quarters of 2013, those figures have fallen to 29% and 13%, respectively (Primack, 2013). Additionally, there have been more VC-backed IPOs in 2013 than in any other year since 2000 (Primack, 2013).

Conclusion

Corporations believe in the success of their dream, and they expect their ventures to take off and expand. One of the greatest challenges for new ventures is the ability to secure capital for investments that will allow the company to grow. All projects will reach a crossroad where sufficient cash flow is necessary in order to go to the next level. It could be after a period of time or it could be because the venture was so popular and the company is growing at a rapid rate due to demand. Regardless of the situation, the company's management team will need to determine when and how they will invest in items such as purchasing new equipment, hiring new staff and putting more money into marketing initiatives. Raising money can be a difficult task if the company has not established a reputation or is still new.

Securing capital is a choice made after weighing the pros and cons of various options. There are three popular sources for obtaining funding for new ventures: Borrowing from financial institutions, partnering with venture capitalists, and selling equity/ownership in exchange for a share of the revenue (Goel & Hasan, 2004). All financing options can be classified into two categories — debt financing and equity capital.

Debt financing and equity capital options both require the financial professionals of an organization to complete detailed documentation prior to the award of financing. The finance team should be prepared to produce quarterly balance sheets, background information on the company and projections.

The first business venture funds were developed in the mid-1960s, approximately 20 years following the formation of the first institutional venture capital funds (Gompers, 2002). "Since that time, corporate venturing has undergone three boom-or-bust cycles that closely track the independent venture capital sector" (Gompers, 2002, p. 2). It has been found that many corporations will consider entering the corporate venture market when the independent sector starts to show hints of capability and achievement (Gompers & Lerner, 1998).

In order to avoid a "backlash of no cash," a business may determine that selling shares of equity would be the best way to secure working capital. This alternative could alleviate some of the stress associated with starting a new venture as well as provide the company an opportunity to grow at a quicker rate. However, the business will be required to give the investors some control and profits. Angel investors may want to take a role in the company, but the venture capitalists will probably want to remain in the background as a silent partner. If the venture is not successful, the investor loses. Therefore, angel investors and venture capitalists will probably require a higher return on investment than a conventional lender since the risks are greater.

Terms & Concepts

Angel Investors: Angel or Angel Investor defines an individual who offers capital to startup businesses in need of added value. Angel investors often boost the companies' financial worth due to their connections and expertise in the field.

Capital: Capital is the combination of all durable investment goods, which are usually added and calculated with units of money.

Commercial Banks: A corporation that receives deposits, offers business loans, and other similar services. Though commercial banks give their services to individual citizens, they usually invest more of their efforts to lending money to and taking deposits from companies.

Cure Period: A cure period is often outlined in a contract, offering a defaulting party to readjust the cause of a default. For instance, cure period if a certain amount of time allowed for the owner to find a solution to a problem that has occurred in the operation of a business.

Debt Financing: Debt financing occurs when a firm advancing its capital through the means of selling bonds to individuals or institutions who are willing to invest. In exchange for the money lent, the investors become creditors and expect to be repaid with interest on the debt that was incurred.

Equity Capital: Money invested in a business by owners, stockholders or others who share in profits.

Financial Institutions: A corporation that gathers funds from public organizations and individuals and puts them in other financial assets like deposits, bonds, and loans instead of tangible properties.

Investments: The gathering of a financial product with the assumption and hope that favorable returns will be present over time. Generally, investments refers to the expending of money in order to make a larger sum of money.

Pro-rata Rights: The investor is given the right to maintain ownership in the company through future investment rounds.

Share: A certificate that represents a single unit of possession in a business, mutual fund, or limited partnership.

Small Business Administration: A governmental agency which makes loans to smaller companies.

Start-up: A corporate venture in its first level of growth.

Venture: Venture is often used to refer to a start-up or enterprise business.

Venture Capitalists: A term that defines an investor that gives capital to start-up companies or offers support to small corporations hoping to expand. Capitalists, however, lack any form of access to public funding.

Bibliography

Advani, A. (2006, November 10). Start-up financing trends for 2007. *Entrepreneur.com.* Retrieved April 9, 2007, from http://www.entrepreneur.com/money/financing/startupfinancingcolumnistasheeshadvani/article170218.html

Advani, A. (2006, October 12). Raising money from informal investors. *Entrepreneur.com.* Retrieved April 9, 2007, from http://www.entrepreneur.com/money/financing/startupfinancingcolumnistasheeshadvani/article168860.html

Capital sources for your business. (2006). *University of Maine Cooperative Extension, Bulletin # 3008.* Retrieved April 9, 2007, from http://www.umext.maine.edu/onlinepubs/htmpubs/3008.htm

Colla, P., Ippolito, F., & Li, K. (2013). Debt specialization. *Journal of Finance, 68*(5), 2117-2141. Retrieved November 24, 2013, from EBSCO Online Database Business Source Complete. http://search.ebscohost.com/login.aspx?direct=true&db=bth&AN=90167647&site=ehost-live

Edelhauser, K. (2007, April 11). Angel investing to grow in '07. *Entrepreneur.com.* Retrieved April 11, 2007, from http://www.entrepreneur.com/blog/entry/176926.html

Goel, R. K., & Hasan, I. (2004). Funding new ventures: Some strategies for raising early finance. *Applied Financial Economics, 14*(11), 773-778. Retrieved on April 9, 2007, from EBSCO Online Database Business Source Complete. http://search.ebscohost.com/login.aspx?direct=true&db=bth&AN=13867653&site=ehost-live

Gompers, P. A. (1995). Optimal investment, monitoring, and the staging of venture capital. *Journal of Finance, 50*(5), 1461-1490. Retrieved on April 9, 2007, from EBSCO Online Database Business Source Complete. http://search.ebscohost.com/login.aspx?direct=true&db=bth&AN=9601031352&site=ehost-live

Gompers, P. (2002). Corporations and the financing of innovation: The corporate venturing experience. *Economic Review, 87*(4), 1. Retrieved October 24, 2007, from EBSCO Online Database Business Source Complete. http://search.ebscohost.com/login.aspx?direct=true&db=bth&AN=8969400&site=ehost-live

Gompers, P., & Lerner, J. (1996). The use of covenants: An empirical analysis of venture partnership agreements. *Journal of Law & Economics, 39*(2), 463-498. Retrieved October 16, 2007, from EBSCO Online Database Business Source Complete. http://search.ebscohost.com/login.aspx?direct=true&db=bth&AN=11511897&site=ehost-live

Kline, A. (2013). Banks urged to team up with microlenders. *American Banker, 178*(165), 13. Retrieved November 24, 2013, from EBSCO Online Database Business Source Complete. http://search.ebscohost.com/login.aspx?direct=true&db=bth&AN=91684938&site=ehost-live

Madill, J., Haines Jr., G., & Rlding, A. (2005). The role of angels in technology SMEs: A link to venture capital. *Venture Capital, 7*(2), 107-129. Retrieved April 14, 2007, from EBSCO Online Database Business Source Complete. http://search.ebscohost.com/login.aspx?direct=true&db=bth&AN=16968283&site=ehost-live

Pierce, C. (2005). How to prepare and present a successful business funding request. Retrieved April 10, 2007, from http://www.businessfinance.com/books/workbook.pdf

Primack, D. (2013). Behind the VC numbers: higher prices, less control. *Fortune.com,* 1. Retrieved November 24, 2013, from EBSCO Online Database Business Source Complete. http://search.ebscohost.com/login.aspx?direct=true&db=bth&AN=91541840&site=ehost-live

Suggested Reading

Atanasova, C. (2007). Access to institutional finance and the use of trade credit. *Financial Management (2000), 36*(1), 49-67. Retrieved October 25, 2007, from EBSCO Online Database Business Source Complete.

Claessens, S., & Tzioumis, K. (2006). Ownership and financing structures of listed and large non-listed corporations. *Corporate Governance: An International Review, 14*(4), 266-276. Retrieved October 16, 2007, from EBSCO Online Database Business Source Complete. http://search.ebscohost.com/login.aspx?direct=true&db=bth&AN=21437470&site=ehost-live

O'Leary, C. (2004). Corporate financing thrives amid modest rate hikes. *Bank Loan Report, 19*(38), 1-11. Retrieved October 16, 2007, from EBSCO Online Database Business Source Complete. http://search.ebscohost.com/login.aspx?direct=true&db=bth&AN=14613650&site=ehost-live

Platt, G. (2006). Corporate financing focus: Fed's shift from automatic to neutral leaves next move up in the air, analysts say. *Global Finance, 20*(6), 65-67. Retrieved October 25, 2007, from EBSCO Online Database Business Source Complete. http://search.ebscohost.com/login.aspx?direct=true&db=bth&AN=21276386&site=ehost-live

Essay by Marie Gould

Marie Gould is an Associate Professor and the Faculty Chair of the Business Administration Department at Peirce College in Philadelphia, Pennsylvania. She teaches in the areas of management, entrepreneurship, and international business. Although Ms. Gould has spent her career in both academia and corporate, she enjoys helping people learn new things — whether it's by teaching, developing or mentoring.

Financial Incentives

Table of Contents

Abstract
Overview
    Why Work?
    Maslow's Hierarchy of Needs
    Importance of Financial Incentives
    Types of Financial Incentive Plans
    Variable Pay Plans
    Piecework Pay Plans
    Bonuses, Stock Options & Profit Sharing
    Merit Pay
    Pay for Performance
Applications
    Financial Incentives within the Sales Industry
    Defining Criteria for Success
    Outcome-Based Standards
    Behavior-Based Standards
Conclusion
Terms & Concepts
Bibliography
Suggested Reading

Abstract

Most organizations use financial incentives to motivate their employees to exude higher performance in support of organizational goals and objectives. On an individual basis, financial incentives include piecework programs, bonuses, promotions, and merit pay raises to encourage consistent above average performance. On a broader level, financial incentives can be given to all employees according to the profitability of the organization; an act which encourages employees to harbor a vested interest in the organization's success. No matter the type of financial incentive used, it must be tied to performance in order to ensure that the employee is fairly compensated and that the organization reaches the high performance it needs and desires.

Overview

Why Work?

Many of us have a love/hate relationship with our jobs. While on some days we can barely drag ourselves out of bed to go to work, on other days the thought of the tasks to be done is so invigorating that we cannot wait to get started. One is truly fortunate if the latter type of mornings outnumber the former. However, all too often this does not seem to be the case. Yet, we still continue to go to work if for no other reason than that we need the paycheck.

Maslow's Hierarchy of Needs

A number of observers have posited various motivations to explain why people work. Although some theorists have tried to reduce motivation to an equation that connects the probability of increased performance with such things as the employee's perceived expectancy of obtaining a reward for doing so, other theorists have posited that different people are motivated by different things such as having one's physical needs met (e.g., food on the table and a roof over one's head), a need for the esteem of others, or some other internal incentive. Abraham Maslow, for example, described a hierarchy of needs ranging from meeting basic physiological needs (e.g., food, clothing, shelter) to safety, belongingness, and esteem needs and eventually self-actualization (see Figure 1). According to this theory, people are motivated by different things depending on where there are on the hierarchy at any given point. For example, a person who has earned a high level position in his/her career and has adequate income for whatever s/he wants to do may be able to focus on self-actualization. However, if that same person loses his/her job or investments, s/he may once again be concerned about meeting basic physiological needs.

Figure 1: Maslow's Hierarchy of Needs

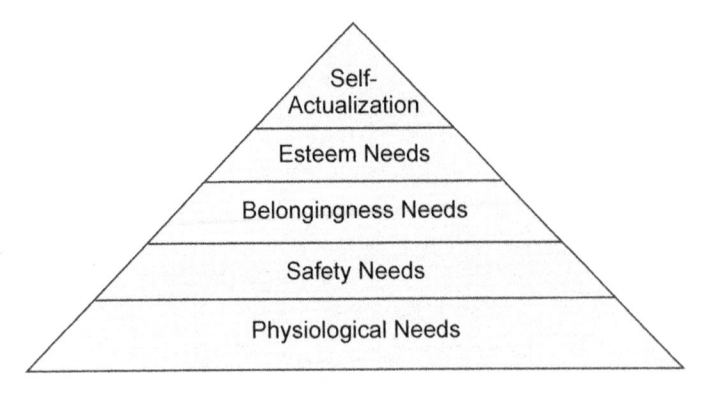

- Self-Actualization
- Esteem Needs
- Belongingness Needs
- Safety Needs
- Physiological Needs

Importance of Financial Incentives

Although virtually every organization tries to motivate its employees through financial incentives, these are not seen as motivators in the scientifically used meaning of the word. Rather, at various places on the hierarchy of needs (or other motivation theory), financial incentives give people the means by which they can meet their needs. For example, in Maslow's hierarchy of needs, a person who is out of work and fears losing his/her house could probably be easily motivated to work for a financial reward that would help him/her put food on the table or pay the mortgage. Once such immediate needs have been met, however, money or other financial incentives allow the person to meet his/her safety needs through such things as obtaining a steady job that brings in a sufficient and reliable paycheck, one's belongingness needs by providing a high enough income to allow the person to be identified with other successful people (either at the work place or through other fee-based institutions like country clubs). Money can also be used to help meet one's esteem needs as people look at the situation that money has allowed the person to attain.

No matter the theory, however, most motivation theorists recognize the fact that most people working in organizations both need and expect remuneration. Sometimes financial incentives are required to meet basic physical needs or to have the security of knowing that those needs will continue to be met for the foreseeable future. In other cases, financial incentives in the form of bonuses, raises, or promotions fill a need for recognition from others. However, no matter what motivators an employee has, from the employee's point-of-view, pay is always a consideration. Although job titles and other perquisites can be important motivators, in most cases employees need more from the organization than to know that they are helping it succeed. To motivate employees to perform at a consistently high level, the organization must give them what they want or need. In most cases, this is some kind of financial incentive that, in turn, allows the employee to obtain or work towards the reward that s/he really wants. One of the things that successful organizations do to motivate employees to contribute to the company's high performance is to link the desired performance to rewards.

The truth is that money and other financial incentives are one of the reasons why people in Western culture work. Although many of us could keep ourselves mentally and physically engaged through other activities, if one does not have the financial status to meet one's needs, a job is the most typical solution. Although other perquisites (e.g., a corner office, a more important title) can be used to reward an employee in the workplace, because of the flexibility of financial incentives to meet one's needs, they are one of the most frequently used rewards. However, to be effective in motivating the kind on the job behavior that will most effectively support the business, the financial incentives need to be linked to job performance. Otherwise, rather than reinforcing the type of behavior that supports the organization, the financial incentives can actually reinforce behavior that is contrary to the good of the organization. For example, one of the reasons that the piecework approach to paying assembly line workers has historically been so widely used is because it ties the financial remuneration that the worker receives to the number of widgets that the worker produces. The more widgets (that are within specification) that the worker produces, the more the worker gets paid under this method. However, if workers were only paid for the number of widgets that they completed — whether or not they were within the standards for an acceptable widget — the financial incentive might actually encourage the workers to produce more widgets that were unacceptable, thereby rewarding them for shoddy work and costing the organization money rather than saving it.

Types of Financial Incentive Plans

There are a number of common approaches to financial incentives in business.

Variable Pay Plans

Variable pay incentive plans tie the employee's pay to a predetermined measure of overall profitability for the organization in general or for the specific facility in which the employee works. In profit sharing plans, most of the employees of the organization receive a share of the annual profits of the organization, typically on a one-time, lump sum basis. In profit sharing plans, all employees share in the profitability of the company. Therefore, the more profitable the company is during a given time period, the greater the reward the employee will receive. In theory, therefore, the employee is motivated to do his/her best in order to increase the profitability of the company and, thereby, also increase his/her financial reward. There are several general types of profit sharing plans.

- Under cash plans, a percentage of the profits of the organization (usually 15 to 20 percent) are distributed to workers at regular intervals.

- Under the Lincoln incentive system, employees work in a guaranteed piecework basis and receive a percentage of the total annual profits of the organization based on their merit rating.

- Under deferred profit sharing plans, a predetermined portion of the organization's profits are placed in an account for each employee. These accounts are supervised by a trustee and payment is often deferred until retirement, thereby offering a tax advantage.

However, although profit sharing plans are currently a popular way to provide financial incentives to employees, research on the effectiveness of profit sharing plans — particularly from the point of view of increased profits for the organization — tend to be ambivalent (Dessler, 2005).

Piecework Pay Plans

In addition, there are number of financial incentive programs that are used to motivate employees on an individual basis. Piecework plans are pay systems that are based on the number of items processed by an individual employee during a specified unit of time. This is one of the oldest individual incentive plans, and is still widely used.

- An example of a straight piecework plan would be to pay a worker based on how many widgets the worker produces during an eight hour shift. The more widgets that the worker produces during that time, the more pay the worker receives; a specified amount for each unit s/he completes (e.g., widgets made; sales calls completed).

- Another type of piecework plan is the standard hour plan. Under this type of financial incentive plan, the employee receives a premium that corresponds to the percent by which the employee's performance exceeds the standard. So, for example, if the standard for making widgets is 100 widgets per day and Harvey produces 120 widgets that day, he would receive a 20 percent bonus on top of his standard pay for that day. Although still widely used today, piecework incentive plans have earned a poor reputation in some industries. For example, in the garment industry, workers may be paid based on how many garments they complete. However, in some cases, a worker may not complete sufficient garments during a day in order to meet the minimum-wage standards.

Bonuses, Stock Options & Profit Sharing

Piecework systems, of course, are difficult to implement for professional or creative employees. It would be unreasonable in most situations, for example, to pay a computer programmer based on the number of lines of code s/he produces per day. A few lines of good code are worth much more to the organization than many lines of poor code. Therefore, many organizations offer professional employees financial incentives in the form of such things as bonuses, stock options, and profit sharing.

Merit Pay

Another financial incentive that is widely used is merit pay. This is an increase in salary that is given to an employee based on the employee's individual performance. Merit pay can be given to an employee on a one time, lump sum basis in the form of a bonus for outstanding work. Merit pay raises for outstanding work, on the other hand, become part of the employee's salary and are given on a continuing basis. For example, at his annual review, Harvey's supervisor might determine that Harvey's work was consistently outstanding enough to warrant a pay raise. This merit raise would be added to Harvey's current base salary to become his new base salary from that point on.

Pay for Performance

Another popular approach for motivating desired behavior in high performing organizations is an approach frequently referred to as "pay for performance." In these plans, employees are rewarded financially for high performance and contributing to the organization's goals. This is true not only for workers at the bottom of the organizational structure as is done in piecework plans, but also all the way up to the chief executive officer. Research performed by the government's General Accounting Office (GAO) has found that there a number of factors that make pay for performance incentive plans successful (U.S. General Accounting Office, 2004).

- First, the GAO found that it is important to use objective competencies to assess the quality of the employee's performance. These should be based on empirical research and directly related to the goals of the organization.

- Second, the GAO found that employee performance ratings should be translated into pay increases or awards so that employees can see a direct, positive consequence for their actions.

- Third, the GAO found that both the employee's current salary and contribution to the organization should be considered when making decisions about compensation, so that rewards for similar contributions are equitable.

- Finally, to be successful and to prevent possible abuse, the GAO found that pay for performance systems should be clear and well-published so that employees know the basis on which decisions are made and what kind of awards are made across the organization.

Applications

Financial Incentives within the Sales Industry

Although financial incentives are used across industries and at all organizational levels, one of the first groups for which financial incentives often springs to mind is sales personnel. Typically, sales personnel are paid a regular salary, on the basis of commission, or some combination of the two plans. In the straight salary approach, the sales person is paid a salary (with occasional incentives) just as is done with most employees. This approach to remunerating sales personnel is particularly appropriate when the salesperson is required to generate leads in addition to making a sale or when the sales job involves customer service in addition to straight sales. Although salary plans are simple to administrate, they have the disadvantage of not linking pay to performance. As a result, members of the sales staff have no particular incentive to become high performing employees. Commission plans, on the other hand, pay sales persons only for results. Under this plan, the salesperson does not receive a regular salary, but is paid only on commission, a set fee or percentage of the sale. However, although commission plans have the advantage of motivating high performance, not every salesperson has the skills and abilities necessary to excel at sales. This can not only lead to dissatisfaction with the plan (and, by extension, the job), but also lead to burnout. Because of the drawbacks of both the straight salary and straight commission approach to remunerating sales employees, most organizations use a plan that is a combination of the two approaches, giving salespersons both a steady salary as well as a commission on any sales made. Most organizations use an 80/20 split between percent of pay coming from base salary and from commissions, although other combinations are also possible.

Defining Criteria for Success

However, although tying the performance of a salesperson to his/her performance makes sense, defining the criteria of success to which financial incentives are attached for a sales job can be a challenging exercise. Two general approaches to linking pay to sales performance have been widely implemented.

Outcome-Based Standards

The first of these is the outcome-based system that focuses on the final outcomes of the sales process (e.g., whether or not a sale was made, total revenues earned by a salesperson in a given period of time). Outcome-based standards tend to be both objective and clear: Either a sales quota was met or it was not. Outcome-based systems tend to be easy to implement because of the relative availability of criteria against which performance can be measured (e.g., number of sales made or dollar volume earned within a given performance assessment period). However, because sales jobs tend to be performed in isolation, it is easy for sales personnel to actually harm the organization while still making a sale (e.g., a salesperson might skimp on customer service and follow-up in order to make another sale or focus on selling more items with a smaller price tag or on items or services that have been proven easier to sell). Outcome-based control systems do not take into account a number of factors that affect the success of a salesperson. Sales often occur over a period of time, particularly when the decision to purchase is a complicated or major one. Further, for many sales personnel, making the sale is only part of the job; the salesperson is also often required to perform customer service not only to make the sale but also after the sale has been made. As a result, it can be difficult to tell whether a salesperson is not doing his/her job well or if s/he is immersed in associated activities that will bear fruit later.

Behavior-Based Standards

Because of the problems with outcome-based control systems arising from the nature of the sales job, many experts argue in favor of a behavior-based rather than an outcome-based control system for sales personnel. Behavior-based systems focus more on the behavior of the sales person rather than his/her final sales. Although these systems better link pay to performance, they also require significantly more monitoring of both the activities and the results of the sales force's efforts. Behavior-based control systems are also more dependent than outcome-based control systems on the knowledge, skills, and abilities that the salesperson brings to the job (e.g., aptitudes, personality traits, general or specific product knowledge), the activities of the sales force (e.g., number of calls made), and the sales strategies employed in trying to make a sale (Anderson & Oliver, 1987). However, although behavior-based control systems overcome a number of the disadvantages associated with outcome-based control systems, they also tend to be complex to develop and implement and more subjective than outcome-based systems. This can lead to employee dissatisfaction and work against the very motivation that it was meant to establish.

Conclusion

Virtually every organization uses some sort of financial incentive to motivate high performance from its employees in support of the organization's goals and objectives. Financial incentives can be as simple as paying the employee for each unit of work performed or as complicated as a package that pays the employee on a combination of salary and reward for either individual or team performance. However, to be effective, financial incentives need to be linked with performance in order to ensure not only that the employee is fairly compensated, but also that the organization is paying for high performance in support of its goals and objectives.

Terms & Concepts

Commission: A set fee or percentage of the sale that is given to a sales representative for convincing a customer to make a purchase.

Control System: The method by which an organization properly compensates its employees; involves supervision, instruction, and appraisal.

Criterion: A dependent or predicted measure that is used to judge the effectiveness of persons, organizations, treatments, or predictors. The ultimate criterion measures effectiveness after all the data are in. Intermediate criteria estimate this value earlier in the process. Immediate criteria estimate this value based on current values.

Empirical: Theories or evidence that are derived from, or based on, observation or experiment.

Hierarchy of Needs: A theory of motivation developed by Abraham Maslow. According to Maslow, there are five levels of need: Physiological, safety, belongingness, esteem, and self-actualization. The theory posits that people's behavior is motivated by where they are in the hierarchy. People can move up and down the hierarchy and can also experience needs from several levels at once.

Incentive: An inducement or reward that is used to motivate an employee to perform a desired action or behave in a manner that supports the organization's goals and objectives. A financial incentive is an incentive that is monetary or financial in nature, such as a pay raise, bonus, or stock options.

Merit Pay: An increase in salary that is given to an employee based on the employee's individual performance. Merit pay can be given to an employee on a one time, lump sum basis in the form of a bonus for outstanding work. Merit pay raises given for consistent outstanding work, on the other hand, become part of the employee's salary and are given on a continuing basis.

Motivation: The needs and thought process that determine a person's behavior. Motivating factors do not necessarily remain constant, but may change with the individual's current circumstances.

Pay for Performance: An incentive plan in which employees are rewarded financially for high performance and contributing to the organization's goals. Pay for performance plans are applicable to all levels within the organization.

Performance Assessment: The process of evaluating an employee's work performance and providing feedback on how well s/he is doing (typically against some standard of performance for that job).

Perquisites ("perks"): Something given to the employee in return for work over and above regular pay or compensation. Perks may include such things as health insurance, a company car, or a private office.

Piecework: A pay system that is based on the number of items processed by an individual employee during a specified unit of time.

Reinforcement: An act, process, circumstance, or condition that increases the probability of a person repeating a response.

Self-Actualization: The need to live up to one's full and unique potential. Associated with self-actualization are such concepts as wholeness, perfection, or completion; a divestiture of "things" in preference to simplicity, aliveness, goodness, and beauty; and a search for meaning in life. In Maslow's hierarchy of needs, this is the ultimate level of motivator for behavior.

Bibliography

Anderson, E. & Oliver, R. L. (1987). Perspectives on behavior-based versus outcome-based salesforce control systems. *Journal of Marketing, 51*(4), 76-88. Retrieved February 17, 2009, from EBSCO Online Database Business Source Complete. http://search.ebscohost.com/login.aspx?direct=true&db=bth&AN=4996249&site=ehost-live

Dessler, G. (2005). *Human resource management* (10th ed.). Upper Saddle River, NJ: Pearson/Prentice Hall.

U.S. General Accounting Office. (2004). *Human capital: Implementing pay for performance at selected personnel demonstration projects* (GAO-04-83). Retrieved March 27, 2007, from EBSCO Online Database Business Source Complete. http://search.ebscohost.com/login.aspx?direct=true&db=bth&AN=18173828&site=ehost-live

Suggested Reading

Atul, M., Gupta, N., & Jenkins, G. D. Jr. (2007). A drop in the bucket: When is a pay raise a pay raise? *Journal of Organizational Behavior, 18*(2), 117-137. Retrieved March 2, 2009, from EBSCO Online Database Business Source Complete. http://search.ebscohost.com/login.aspx?direct=true&db=bth&AN=12493230&site=ehost-live

Darmon, R. Y. (1987). The impact of incentive compensation on the salesperson's work habits: An economic model. *Journal of Personal Selling and Sales Management, 7*(1), 21-32. Retrieved March 2, 2009, from EBSCO Online Database Business Source Complete. http://search.ebscohost.com/login.aspx?direct=true&db=bth&AN=6652095&site=ehost-live

Kahn, L. M. & Sherer, P. D. (1990). Contingent pay and managerial performance. *Industrial and Labor Relations Review, 43*(3), 107S-120S. Retrieved March 2, 2009, from EBSCO Online Database Business Source Complete. http://search.ebscohost.com/login.aspx?direct=true&db=bth&AN=9603275758&site=ehost-live

Palia, D., Abraham, R. S., & Wang, C.-J. (2008). Founders versus no-founders in large companies: Financial incentives and the call for regulation. *Journal of Regulatory Economics, 33*(1), 55-86. Retrieved March 2, 2009, from EBSCO Online Database Business Source Complete. http://search.ebscohost.com/login.aspx?direct=true&db=bth&AN=27978131&site=ehost-live

Peterson, S. J. & Luthans, F. (2006). The impact of financial and nonfinancial on business-unit outcomes over time. *Journal of Applied Psychology, 91*(1), 156-165. Retrieved March 2, 2009, from EBSCO Online Database Business Source Complete. http://search.ebscohost.com/login.aspx?direct=true&db=bth&AN=19504997&site=ehost-live

Essay by Ruth A. Wienclaw

Dr. Ruth A. Wienclaw holds a Ph.D. in industrial/organizational psychology with a specialization in organization development from the University of Memphis. She is the owner of a small business that works with organizations in both the public and private sectors, consulting on matters of strategic planning, training, and human/systems integration.

Cash Flow

Table of Contents

Abstract

Overview
- History of Business Cash Flow Reporting

Applications
- FASB Statement 95
- Current Challenges to Companies Managing Cash Flow
- Strategies

Issues
- Benefits of Forecasting
- New Technology
- Centralized Forecasting
- Compliance
- New Statistical & Economic Analyses
- Cash Flow at Risk (CFaR)
- Private Equity & Firm Debt
- Payment Systems

Conclusion

Terms & Concepts

Bibliography

Suggested Reading

Abstract

This essay covers important topics related to the management of cash flow within companies. Cash is defined as currency in corporate accounts, short term investments or commercial paper that's easily convertible to cash. A steady cash flow enables a business to pay its employees and vendors and to invest in new projects and opportunities. Companies face many risks associated with running out of cash; without a ready supply of cash, businesses cannot replay loans, provide goods and services to customers or invest in future growth opportunities. Businesses are required to file a statement of cash flow as outlined by the Financial Accounting Standard's Board Statement of Cash Flow (FASB statement 95). Trends in cash management are evolving to meet the opportunities offered by global markets and to mitigate risks associated with cash shortfalls. Emerging topics in cash management include more active methods of forecasting company cash flow. Other factors that will impact cash management forecasting include: Improved technology, centralization of corporate forecasting, tighter regulatory controls, and new statistical techniques for cash flow analysis.

Overview

Without the proper accounting of cash flow intake and outflow over time, businesses would be operating at great risk of coming up short on liquid capital. Having a tally of cash on-hand, what's coming in (accounts receivable) and what's going out (accounts payable), allows a business to meet expenses and plan future operations. Depending upon the size and complexity of the business operation, a firm is likely to want to project future cash flow in the short-term (12 months) or long-term (5-10 years). Small business with limited access to credit may find that they must forecast cash flow needs for a number of weeks or months. In all cases, cash flow management requires planning and projections into the future and should take into account reasonable risks that might cause a company to fall short of cash.

History of Business Cash Flow Reporting

Originally, businesses were required to file a statement of changes in financial position, or a funds statement. In 1961, Accounting Research Study No. 2, sponsored by the American Institute of Certified Public Accountants (AICPA), recommended that a funds statement be included with the income statement and balance sheet in annual reports to shareholders.

By 1963, the Accounting Principles Board (APB) had issued its Opinion No. 3 as a guideline to help with preparation of the funds statement. While the funds statement was not mandatory for many, businesses saw its value and began to use it regularly. In 1971, Opinion No. 19 (Reporting Changes in Financial Position), also issued by the APB designated the funds statement as one of the three primary financial documents required in annual reports to shareholders. The APB also said a funds statement must be covered by the auditor's report, but did not specify a particular format for the funds statement.

That flexibility came to an end in late 1987, with the Financial Accounting Standards Board's (FASB) issuance of Statement No. 95, which called for a statement of cash flows to replace the more general funds statement. Additionally, the FASB, in an effort to help investors and creditors better predict future cash flow, specified a universal statement format that highlighted cash flow from operating, investing, and financing activities. This format is still used today (Managing Your Cash Flow, 2005).

Cash flow statements provide essential information to company owners, shareholders and investors and provide an overview of the status of cash flow at a given point in time. Cash flow management is an ongoing process that ties the forecasting of cash flow to strategic goals and objectives of an organization.

This article outlines some of the most common strategies, challenges and issues related to managing cash flow. Issues and challenges include: Maintaining good customer and vendor relations while managing accounts payable and receivable, and paying close attention to the time lag between cash inflows and outflows.

The newest trends in cash management forecasting are also covered in detail. Current methods of forecasting cash flow typically involve the use of regression techniques which don't take into account many business operational variables. This essay details some of the current trends in cash flow forecasting that involve improved computer applications, new statistical methods, the centralization of the forecasting function and other significant developments.

Applications

FASB Statement 95

FASB Statement 95 *Statement of Cash Flows* governs the format of a business's reporting of cash flow. Statement 95 encourages enterprises to report cash flows from operating activities directly by showing major classes of operating cash receipts and payments (the direct method). Enterprises that choose not to show operating cash receipts and payments are required to report the same amount of net cash flow from operating activities indirectly by adjusting net income to reconcile it to net cash flow from operating activities (the indirect or reconciliation method) (FASB, 2007).

The following are cash flow measurements required by the FASB:

- Cash Flow Statements: The cash flow statement acts as a kind of corporate checkbook that reconciles the other two statements. Simply put, the cash flow statement records the company's cash transactions (the inflows and outflows) during the given period.
- Cash Flow from Operating Expenses: Measures the cash used or provided by a company's normal operations. It shows the company's ability to generate consistently positive cash flow from operations. Think of "normal operations" as the core business of the company.
- Cash Flows from Investing Activities: Lists all the cash used or provided by the purchase and sales of income-producing assets.
- Cash Flows from Financing Activities: Measures the flow of cash between a firm and its owners and creditors. Negative numbers can mean the company is servicing debt but can also mean the company is making dividend payments and stock repurchases (Essentials of Cash Flow, 2005).

Cash flow from investment and financing activities are fairly straightforward as outlined by Statement 95. However, Statement 95 allows businesses to report using one of two different methods when it comes to reporting cash flows generated or consumed by operations: The direct method and the indirect method.

- The direct method reports inflows of cash (e.g., from sales) and cash outflows for payment of expenses (e.g., purchases of inventory).
- The indirect method which begins with the net income number, a mixture of cash (e.g., cash proceeds from sales) and non-cash components (e.g., depreciation) and removes non-cash or accrual items, then adjusts for the cash effects of transactions not yet reflected in the income statement (e.g., cash payments for inventory not yet sold).

However, only the direct method reports actual sources and amounts of cash inflows and outflows; the information investors need to understand to evaluate the liquidity, solvency, and long-term viability of a company.

Although the standards generally allow managers to select either method for reporting cash flows, the overwhelming majority have chosen to use the indirect method; the approach that provides the least useful information for investment decisions (Direct- versus Indirect-Method Reporting for Cash Flows, 2007).

Current Challenges to Companies Managing Cash Flow

According to Brian Hamilton, CEO of Sageworks, "Businesses don't fail because they are unprofitable; they fail because they get crushed on the accounts receivable side" (Feldman, 2005).

Companies that run short on cash have to use credit cards or lines of credit to fund operations and pay bills. Lack of cash can cause damage to relationships with vendors and banks result in missed market opportunities, and an overall hit to a company's reputation. Running short of cash can result from poor forecasting, unforeseen risks and poor internal management of cash flow. One of the biggest reasons that businesses run short on cash has to do with unrealistic expectations about how quickly cash will come in the door.

Companies need to be realistic about the length of time it will take to get paid — if one assumes payment in 30 days and it takes 60 days to get the cash, then adjustments to "cash in hand" figures need to be made. Corporations are becoming slower to pay vendors; companies want to make more of their cash which means that they are holding on to it longer. Many businesses are also revising their payables to 45-60 days instead of the previous standard of 30 days (Feldman, 2005).

The lag between the time you have to pay suppliers and employees and the time you collect from customers is the problem. The solution is cash flow management and the idea is to delay outlays of cash as long as possible, while encouraging those who owe you to pay quickly.

Creating a cash flow projection is a preemptive action that is meant to alert a business owner or management to the possibility of a cash crunch before it strikes. Projecting cash flow is not a difficult undertaking, but it does require that accurate and timely information regarding payables and receivables be documented. The following information needs to be considered:

- Customer payment history;
- Assessment of upcoming expenditures;
- Patience of vendors (terms of payment);
- Assume that receivables will arrive at a non-constant rate.

Once the above points have been considered, as accurate a figure for cash inflow and outflow as possible should be calculated.

Gather cash inflow information from salespeople, service representatives, collections, credit workers and your finance department. In all cases, you'll be asking the same question: How much cash in the form of customer payments, interest earnings, service fees, partial collections of bad debts, and other sources are we going to get in, and when?

(How to Better Manage Your Cash Flow, 2003).

Gather cash outflow information. Have a line item on your projection for every significant outlay, including rent, inventory (when purchased for cash), salaries and wages, sales and other taxes withheld or payable, benefits paid, equipment purchased for cash, professional fees, utilities, office supplies, debt payments, advertising, vehicle and equipment maintenance and fuel, and cash dividends (How to Better Manage Your Cash Flow, 2003).

Strategies

There's no question that in today's business environment, cash flow management must be a required company activity. Cash flow management means more than tracking where your dollars are, it also requires working with vendors, partners and bankers to insure that cash is always on hand.

- Set up a line of credit before you need it. Banks are not the only source of credit. Sometimes a company's suppliers are more vested in a company's viability than the bank and may extend payment terms to mitigate a cash shortfall.
- Ask your best customers to accelerate payments and offer a discount if they pay quickly.
- Ask your worst customers to pay and ask them often; offer steep discounts if they are willing to pay up.
- In many cases, negotiated agreements can be worked out with vendors; vendors are managing their cash flow too.
- Consolidate vendors and negotiate more favorable terms — this strategy will allow a company to hold on to working capital longer.

Issues

This article has reviewed some of the challenges that face businesses in managing cash flow. Organizations, both large and small, are becoming adept in cash management practices through better accounting of cash and improved customer and vendor management tactics. The global business landscape demands even greater levels of diligence in tracking company cash flow through cash flow management forecasting. The benefits of deliberate and well planned cash management forecasting cannot be overstated.

Benefits of Forecasting

Precise forecasting can help companies guarantee payments to suppliers on specific dates, allowing a company to secure better credit terms. Another benefit from cash flow forecasting is a firm's ability to optimize working capital. By tightening up payment plans and investment activities, many companies are actually able to minimize the amount of cash they need on hand. Good forecasters are adept at "extracting" cash from operations and improving cash flow. Cash management is about knowing where cash is and when it will be needed. If cash is not going to be needed right away, a savvy forecaster may be able to move cash from one investment area to another and thus create value through higher returns-while still maintaining access to the liquid funds. Another benefit to cash management involves debt. Covenants or restrictions on debt financing often require that a minimum cash balance be maintained. Violations of the covenant could lead to higher interest rates, penalties and loan terminations. Overall, good cash management can help to improve or maintain a company's financial reputation.

New Technology

Spreadsheets have been the predominant cash flow management tool for many years. Analysis of data accuracy on spreadsheets and the analysis reveals that financial data on spreadsheets is highly prone to error. Errors in reporting of company financial information sound alarm bells and makes those who are responsible for corporate compliance very nervous. Large organizations (typically early adopters of new technology) are moving to integrated financial databases such as Treasury Information Systems (TIS). Though the cost of implementation can be significant, improved efficiency and data sharing is a big benefit. Information systems can be shared across networks with multiple users accessing secure information which also makes them a superior choice to spreadsheets. Another option is a web-based treasury module that is incorporated within an ERP (Enterprise Resource Planning) system. Properly integrated treasury functions within an enterprise system can track: Account balances and transactions, cash positions, fund transfers, short-term investments and cash flow forecasts.

Centralized Forecasting

Most cash flow management to-date has been handled at a local business unit level, with each division handling cash management in their own way. The past few years have seen a significant rise in the trend toward centralized cash flow forecasting. The benefits are numerous; from a staffing stand point, it is possible to consolidate cash management personnel from across an enterprise to one central area which cuts down on personnel costs. Increased uniformity and standardization of methodologies is another benefit to centralizing cash management analysis and management. Decentralized reporting of cash flow and forecasting was often completed orally within departments. There has also been a lack of incentive for local divisions to report into a central unit, with many operating in silos. As forecasting becomes a more centralized function, companies will initiate benchmarks to monitor locally provided data and eventually will be used across units to provide incentive to managers to provide accurate and timely data for central forecasting.

Compliance

The requirements of Sarbanes-Oxley (SOX) compliance have generated more and better financial data for forecasting. The generation of more detailed and timely cash flow information was a somewhat unexpected benefit of increased compliance and regulatory laws. Compliance added significantly to the cost of tracking corporate financial data, but the careful monitoring and greater visibility of cash flow for treasury personnel has also been a windfall for increasing the accuracy of forecasting. Treasury Information Systems are becoming an essential tool for storing the growing volume of financial data. Cash flow management data can be extracted out of overall financial data, and be shared more easily. Information systems for tracking company financial data have allowed access by senior managers to data that was formerly hard to access. Integrated financial information systems allow easy access to company financial data for strategic planning purposes.

New Statistical & Economic Analyses

Most firms, to date, have used basic regression techniques to model cash flow forecasting. Regression is a useful model, but makes the assumption that the firm's business won't change over time (Germaise, 2007).

A more flexible and accurate approach to cash flow forecasting is the project-level forecast. This method forecasts cash flow patterns by project which are modeled separately rather than lumped together and reported as a firm-wide forecast. This method has the following advantages:

- Good method for modeling a small number of large projects.
- Good for modeling a changing mix of projects.
- Reveals the impact that larger projects might have on cash flow-this impact can be significant and varies by project.

Once all projects have been modeled, start dates can be estimated and project totals generated to provide a firm-wide forecast as well as the individual-by project.

Driver-based cash flow modeling is acknowledged to be the best forecasting strategy available. Driver-based models model are designed to link central business decisions and risks to financial forecasts. Business drivers are being widely used across organizations to link operational strategy with functional areas such as performance management, sales and finance. Driver-based forecasting for cash flow moved away from a purely financial model and incorporates variables that drive business.

The three main types of drivers that affect cash flow forecasting are:

- Internal: New products, new marketing strategies, expansion. Senior managers can use this information to assess if firm has financial resources to undertake internal initiatives.
- External: Factors outside firm's control such as regulatory changes or competitor price cut.
- External Macroeconomic: Also outside of firm's control such as recession, inflation, increased transportation costs.

Cash Flow at Risk (CFaR)

Cash Flow at Risk (CFaR) is defined as the likelihood that a firm will run out of cash. CFaR is just one of the modeling scenarios that define an entire universe of corporate risk and predict the chance of severe shock in an organization. The CFaR model is focused on the likelihood of risk of a disastrous event that could specifically impact cash flow. CFaR is modeled after the Value at Risk tool that is often used by financial firms to assess risk to their overall portfolios. This model can be used successfully by non-financial firms to predict the likelihood of a liquidity crisis.

Private Equity & Firm Debt

Firms financed by private equity (PE) deals as leveraged buy-outs (LBOs) typically carry a very heavy debt burden, with as much as 60%-80% debt financing. These firms are required to make substantial interest payments and even a small liquidity crunch can spell disaster for a company holding this much debt. Cash flow forecasts keep buyers informed of cash flow risk scenarios. The accuracy of cash flow models in this case is absolutely imperative for buyers to make informed decisions about risk. Multiple cash flow outcome methods should be run to insure that none is overly optimistic or pessimistic; both potentially to making financial decisions. PE managers state that accurate forecasting; along with openness to investors, are the most critical factors in managing cash flow in an LBO. It is a good idea to run cash flow models in times of economic expansion and not wait until an economic downturn; the term "forecast" implies that these models are most useful in predicting future events.

Payment Systems

Several of the trends in cash flow forecasting favor the use of electronic payments and payment cards over checks. Many companies manage cash flow on very tight schedules by holding onto cash as long as possible and encouraging customers to pay quickly. This method helps to keep a maximum of cash on hand. Being able to move funds electronically in and out of cash accounts helps firms stay on top of cash flow.

Some of the benefits are obvious and listed below:

- More timely and predictable schedule;
- More secure transactions;
- Allow for more precise forecasting;
- Can strengthen relationships between vendors/customer by allowing them to manage their own cash flows better.

Conclusion

This paper has discussed many issues related to tracking, managing and reporting business cash flow. All companies are required to submit a statement of cash flow as part of their required financial statement. FASB Statement 95 provides guidelines for reporting cash flow. A Business's *Statement of Cash Flow* reports cash flow in three areas: Business operations, financial activities and investing. Businesses are managing their cash flow very carefully these days. Careful management of accounts receivable and payables is essential in keeping cash on hand. Companies are negotiating better terms with vendors while creating incentives to get customers to pay up.

Businesses operate in global markets and are often open for business 24/7. Cash management forecasting is an essential function within large multinational organizations. Some best practices for cash management forecasting include:

- Technological innovation. Systems move toward an integrated TIS (treasury information system) or ERP.
- Employ driver-based forecasting; simulations or regressions.
- Payment methods. Integrate electronic payment system with customer and supplier accounts.
- Focus treasury staff's attention on analysis of cash flow variability not just data collection.
- Incorporate forecasting into operational planning. Larger firms are doing a better job and a gap is widening between large and S/M enterprises.

Cash shortfalls can be very costly to an organization. Firms that are debt-laden can easily become financially constrained and default on debt payments. Projects may be delayed and new business opportunities can be missed because there's no cash to fund them. Securing emergency lines of credit are expensive; a line of credit should be set in a time when there is no cash crunch. Lastly, having a steady, adequate and predictable cash flow is the best protection against business insolvency and failure.

Terms & Concepts

<u>**Cash:**</u> Refers to currency, checks on hand, and deposits in the bank. Cash equivalents are: Short-term investments, temporary investments (treasury bills, certificate of deposits or commercial paper). Cash equivalents can easily be converted to cash.

<u>**Cash Flow Statement:**</u> Records the company's cash transactions (the inflows and outflows) during the given period. It is one of the four main financial statements of a company. The cash flow statement breaks the sources of cash generation into three sections: Operational cash flows, investing and financing.

<u>**Cash Management Forecasting:**</u> A prediction of the amount of money that will move through an organization.

<u>**FABS Statement 95:**</u> Requires that a statement of cash flows classify cash receipts and payments according to whether they stem from operating, investing, or financing activities and provides definitions of each category (FASB).

Financing Cash Flow: Measures the flow of cash between a firm and its owners and creditors. Negative numbers can mean the company is servicing debt but can also mean the company is making dividend payments and stock repurchases (Essentials of Cash Flow, 2005).

Free Cash Flow (FCF): Refers to cash that is available for distribution among all the security holders of a company. They include equity holders, debt holders, preferred stock holders, convertibles holders, and so on.

Internal Rate of Return (IRR): A capital budgeting method used by firms to decide whether they should make long-term investments. A project is a good investment proposition if its IRR is greater than the rate of return that could be earned by alternative investments (investing in other projects, buying bonds, even putting the money in a bank account).

Investment Cash Flow: Lists all the cash used or provided by the purchase and sale of income-producing assets.

Operating Cash Flow: Measures the cash used or provided by a company's normal operations.

Net Present Value: The difference between the present value of cash inflows and the present value of cash outflows. NPV is used in capital budgeting to analyze the profitability of an investment or project.

Present Value: The current worth or future sum of money or stream of cash flows given a specified rate of return. Future cash flows are discounted at the discount rate, and the higher the discount rate, the lower the present value of the future cash flows.

Regression Analysis: A statistical measure that attempts to determine the strength of the relationship between one dependent variable (usually denoted by Y) and a series of other changing variables (known as independent variables). The two basic types of regression are linear regression and multiple regression (Investopedia, 2007).

Table 1: The table below shows the general format for a statement of cash flow

Cash provided (or used) by:	
Operating activities	$XXX
Investing activities	$XXX
Financing activities	$XXX
Net increase (decrease) in cash and cash equivalents	$XXX
Cash and cash equivalents at beginning of year	$XXX
Cash and cash equivalents at end of year	$XXX

Bibliography

Call, A. C., Chen, S., & Tong, Y. H. (2013). Are analysts' cash flow forecasts naïve extensions of their own earnings forecasts? *Contemporary Accounting Research, 30*(2), 438-465. Retrieved November 15, 2013, from EBSCO Online Database Business Source Complete. http://search.ebscohost.com/login.aspx?direct=true&db=bth&AN=88155561&site=ehost-live

CFA Institute. (2007). Direct- versus indirect-method reporting for cash flows. Retrieved September 27, 2007, from http://www.aimrpubs.org/centre/positions/reporting/direct%5fvs%5findirect.html

Dasgupta, S., Noe, T. H., & Wang, Z. (2011). Where did all the dollars go? the effect of cash flows on capital and asset structure. *Journal of Financial & Quantitative Analysis, 46*(5), 1259-1294. Retrieved November 15, 2013, from EBSCO Online Database Business Source Complete. http://search.ebscohost.com/login.aspx?direct=true&db=bth&AN=67547639&site=ehost-live

The essentials of cash flow. (2005, July 15). Investopedia. Retrieved September 24, 2007, from http://www.investopedia.com/articles/01/110701.asp

Feldman, A. (2005, December). Cash flow crunch. *Inc.com.* Retrieved September 24, 2007, from http://www.inc.com/magazine/20051201/handson-finance.html

Garmaise, M. (2007, September). Optimize business performance through cash flow management. *Visa Commercial.* Retrieved September 24, 2007, from http://www.corporate.visa.com/md/dl/documents/downloads/CashFlowForecasting.pdf?src=sym

Hales, J., & Orpurt, S. F. (2013). A review of academic research on the reporting of cash flows from operations. *Accounting Horizons, 27*(3), 539-578. Retrieved November 15, 2013, from EBSCO Online Database Business Source Complete. http://search.ebscohost.com/login.aspx?direct=true&db=bth&AN=90327375&site=ehost-live

How to better manage your cash flow. (2003, December 11). *Entrepreneur.com.* Retrieved September 24, 2007, from http://www.entrepreneur.com/money/moneymanagement/managingcashflow/article66008.html

Managing your cash flow. (2005). *Virtual Advisor.* Retrieved September 24, 2007, from http://www.va-interactive.com/inbusiness/editorial/finance/ibt/cash%5fflow.html

Wengroff, J. (2001, June 1). Cash management: Forecasting the flow. *CFO.com*. Retrieved September 27, 2007, from http://www.cfo.com/article.cfm/2996251

Suggested Reading

Kagan, P. (2006). Cable kings of cash flow. *CableFAX's CableWORLD, 18*(25), 14-14. Retrieved September 24, 2007, from EBSCO Online Database Business Source Premier. http://search.ebscohost.com/login.aspx?direct=true&db=buh&AN=23327569&site=ehost-live

Kintzele, P. (1990, February). Implementing SFAS 95, statement of cash flows. *The CPA Journal*. Retrieved September 27, 2007, from http://www.nysscpa.org/cpajournal/old/08209170.htm

Krell, E. (2003). BPM accelerates as short-term forecasting slows. *Business Finance*. Retrieved September 27, 2007, from http://www.bfmag.com/magazine/archives/article.html?articleID=13962&pg=1

Weiss, N., & Yang, J. (2007). The cash flow statement: Problems with the current rules. *CPA Journal, 77*(3), 26-31. Retrieved September 24, 2007, from EBSCO Online Database Business Source Premier. http://search.ebscohost.com/login.aspx?direct=true&db=buh&AN=24310856&site=ehost-live

Essay by Carolyn Sprague, MLS

Carolyn Sprague holds a BA degree from the University of New Hampshire and a Masters Degree in Library Science from Simmons College. Carolyn gained valuable business experience as owner of her own restaurant which she operated for 10 years. Since earning her graduate degree Carolyn has worked in numerous library/information settings within the academic, corporate and consulting worlds. Her operational experience as a manger at a global high tech firm and more recent work as a web content researcher have afforded Carolyn insights into many aspects of today's challenging and fast-changing business climate.

Terminal Value

Table of Contents

- Abstract
- Overview
  - Importance of Valuation
  - Discounted Cash Flow
- Applications
  - Asset-based Approach
  - Comparable Market-based Valuation Method
  - Capitalization Models
  - Discounted Cash Flow Method
- Issues
  - Life Cycle & Firm Survival
  - Merger & Acquisition or Investment Valuation Methodologies
  - Non-Financial Variables for Valuation
  - Weighted Average Cost of Capital (WACC)
  - Benefits of the DCF Valuation Method
- Conclusion
- Terms & Concepts
- Bibliography
- Suggested Reading

Abstract

Terminal value is one component of determining the overall value of a given enterprise. Terminal value can be estimated in three ways: Liquidation values, exit multiples approach or stable growth model. Terminal value is calculated to project the value of an entity (security or firm) at a future date in time-taking into consideration future cash flow at a discounted rate for a several year period. The discounted cash flow (DCF) method is examined in detail in this essay as one of the most widely employed methods for calculating terminal value. The DCF method of valuation is used in conjunction with rates of stable growth within companies after periods of high growth. Terminal values can represent a large part of the valuation of a firm and can be calculated for individual assets of a business or the business as a whole. This essay also reviews the topic of business valuation as a broader topic and identifies why the determination of the value of a firm is important to different stakeholders. The impact of company life-cycle growth and Mergers and Acquisitions will also be examined in the valuation context.

Overview

The process of arriving at a business' value must include a detailed and comprehensive analysis that includes factors such as, past, present and future earnings and overall prospects of the company. Earnings figures offer tangible metrics with which to calculate a company's performance over time and thus contribute to assigning a value to a company. When considering additional criteria such as "overall company prospects" in business valuation, there is a much greater probability that different judgments will yield different assessments of business valuation. Business valuation can be determined using a number of methods, each with its own set of variables which result in a wide variance in determining business valuation. "The primary difference among the various valuation approaches is attributable to the method in which those benefits are estimated. Controversy exists among valuation practitioners and academics as to which methods are most appropriate, as evidenced by, among other things, the substantial amount of litigation and other legal proceedings surrounding valuation issues" (Jenkins, 2006).

Importance of Valuation

Valuation of a corporation or business is important in a number of contexts. Valuation may be used to determine how much a company is worth as a going concern (operating company). If a company is being acquired, it is also critical to determine the value at which the acquisition makes good financial sense. Another scenario might involve determining the value of a business that is facing financial distress. Determining value for a company is not easy, nor is it an exact science. Much of the process of valuation is judgment-based, and poor decisions can result in a poor investment or financing decisions. The purpose of valuation provides the overall framework for management to make informed decisions. Corporate managers might be faced with several different contexts for valuation including sale, liquidation, acquisition or bailout (Giddy, 2006).

A business's value can be determined using different valuation models and variables.

The three broad approaches to estimating value are (Jenkins, 2006):

- Asset-based- determines the value of collective assets.
- Income-based- estimates future income streams (DCF- discounted cash flow method).
- Market based- uses market multiples of assets and income.

It is not realistic to assume that a firm will always be in business; many firms do fail. In such a case, a company's assets would be appraised and liquidated. The price realized after payment of outstanding debt would reflect the valuation of the business.

Discounted Cash Flow

This essay focuses primarily on the use of discounted cash flow (DCF) as a means of business value. The DCF valuation method ultimately calculates a terminal value for a business and is based on future operating results. DCF is considered the preferred tool to value a business and assumes that the company will continue to operate in the future. Future benefits to owners of a business are widely accepted as the value in owning a company. In order to determine the future value (acquisition price) of a business, it is necessary to project what value stream will be available in the future. DCF is based on projected future operating results, rather than historical results (Valuation Methodologies, 2005).

Mergers and acquisitions have been prevalent in recent years as more corporations expand into global markets. Having a realistic idea of the value that a business merger or acquisition can provide has become imperative in competitive markets. Investors rely on business valuation to project the future benefits and terminal values that influence where their investment dollars will go. A business valuation of the target (acquired) firm is required as part of the acquisition process and can have a significant affect on purchase prices and financing decisions. This paper discusses the role of DFC methods in determining the value of a target firm as well as other factors that influence the value and acquisition.

Applications

There are three general methods for determining, or estimating, the value of a business. They are:

- Asset-based;
- Comparable market-based;
- Income-based.

Asset-based Approach

An asset-based valuation method requires the appraisal of a company's assets and liabilities to determine their value in the current market. The appraisal may be done at a discrete level (individual assets) or collectively. It is often necessary to employ a specialist with specific industry knowledge to assign value to assets. The value of the assets is assumed to come from future income. Assets can generate income through their potential use or from their liquidation value.

Comparable Market-based Valuation Method

There are two different market-based valuations that are commonly used to ascertain business value: The comparison of similar transactions and the comparison of similar public companies.

- **Transactions** The analysis of financial and operating data from other similar transactions can be applied to a target company to predict value. The comparison is based on historical data and compares companies in similar lines of business to establish a price for the target firm.
- **Public Companies Method** This method uses benchmarks from existing public companies to determine business value for firms that are comparable to the target firm. Firms in publicly traded markets can be benchmarked by stock prices and provide nearly "real-time" views of markets. This method requires that investors see targets and comparables as similar to gain investor confidence.

In each of the above comparable market-based value methods, premiums or discounts may be applied to the valuation to reflect strengths/growth opportunities or weaknesses/challenges of the given target.

- **Income Approach** Business valuation using an income method requires two things: A reasonable estimate of the expected future benefits and an appropriate discount rate. The appropriate discount rate allows for the conversion of the future income to present day value.

The most common methods of estimating value have traditionally involved the discounting or capitalizing of an income stream. In the income approach, variables such as earnings or cash flows are utilized as a proxy for the expected benefits to the owners of the business. Common examples of valuation methods under the income approach are the earnings capitalization model and the discounted cash flows (DCF) model (Valuation Methodologies, 2005).

Capitalization Models

In a capitalization model, a representative level of income is capitalized into perpetuity at a capitalization rate determined by the difference between the appropriate discount rate and a constant, sustainable level of growth (i.e., a price-to-earnings multiple).

The primary difference between discounting and capitalizing is the level of discretion afforded in controlling the growth of the income stream. In any case, reasonable growth assumptions and an appropriate discount rate are imperative for effective valuation.

In a discounting model, a projection of income is estimated for a finite period, followed by a terminal value calculation that assumes a constant income growth rate from that point into perpetuity (Valuation Methodologies, 2005).

Discounted Cash Flow Method

Discounted cash flow methodology is the preferred method for business valuation. This method is also a good one to employ when considering straight investment opportunities. It is important to remember that the goal of DCF valuation is to compute the present day value of cash flow over the life of a company. Put another way, this valuation is a way to project in terms of today's dollars, what a company will be worth in the future (5-10 years out). The analysis is broken into the two distinct parts that have already been discussed in this essay:

- Determine a forecast period (5-10 years) and predict free cash flow for that interval of time. Forecast periods may vary, but generally speaking, the forecast period will equate to the period of time that a firm can expect to enjoy competitive advantage. After the forecast period (x # of years), it is expected that the company will enter a period of stable growth-also known as a "steady state."
- The terminal value of the firm is calculated after the forecast period and once it is assumed that the company is in a steady state. A terminal value is captured at that point and WACC (weighted average cost of capital) is used to discount the terminal value into present value (value of company it today's dollars).

Stable GrowthAs a firm grows, it becomes more difficult for it to maintain high growth and it eventually will grow at a rate less than or equal to the growth rate of the economy in which it operates. This growth rate, labeled stable growth, can be sustained in perpetuity, allowing us to estimate the value of all cash flows beyond that point as a terminal value for a going concern (Damodaran, 2002).

Determining how and when a company might transition to stable growth directly impacts terminal value. A stable growth rate can occur in two general ways. The growth rate of a company will drop abruptly and equalize at a stable rate or growth will diminish over time and stabilize.

Factors that will impact a firm's transition to stable growth are:
- Firm size (relative to the market it serves);
- Current growth rate;
- Competitive advantage.

Issues

Life Cycle & Firm Survival

Companies that have achieved stable growth tend to be more mature firms that have been around for a while. A company that has achieved stable growth may or may not have been in a high growth cycle at some time in its existence. In today's marketplace, there are many firms that enjoy an almost meteoric rise in certain markets. As was emphasized earlier in this essay, rates of high growth are not sustainable indefinitely and companies tend to mature into a stable rate of growth.

"There is a link between where a firm is in the life cycle and survival. Young firms with negative earnings and cash flows can run into serious cash flow problems and end up being acquired by firms with more resources at bargain basement prices. Why are new technology firms more exposed to this problem? The negative cash flows from operations, when combined with significant reinvestment needs, can result in rapid depletion of cash reserves. A widely used measure of the potential for a cash flow problem for firms with negative earnings is the cash-burn ratio, which is estimated as the cash balance of the firm divided by its earnings before interest, taxes and depreciation- known as (EBITDA) (Damodaran, 2002).

Merger & Acquisition or Investment Valuation Methodologies

Companies that are targets of M&A are very often firms that are projected to have a period of high growth. In other cases, acquisition targets are seen as being very complementary to the acquiring firm. In any case, a number of high profile mergers and acquisitions have been documented; the following discussion centers on business valuation within the M&A context.

Of particular note in the M&A scenario are variables to valuing a company that can't be calculated directly or that are subjective and therefore alter valuation results. In the case of a merger, there are always at least two parties involved in the transaction; sometimes more. The first participant is the acquirer (bidder or buyer) and the second is the target firm (seller or acquired). One of the most fundamental questions for any acquirer is the following: Would the target company be a good investment? As with general business valuations and associated analysis, there are a number of questions that, once answered, can help with the valuation of a target company.

Non-Financial Variables for Valuation

The following are number non-financial statement variables that must be taken into consideration when completing a business valuation regardless of the valuation method used.

- There is proprietary technology in the target company. The target has a particular skill or expertise.
- There is a strong market position for the target company.
- The target company has an extensive sales network that will insure future revenue.

- There's an experienced management team at the target company and many will remain at target.
- There are cost savings to be gained from the merger.
- Synergies between the two merging firms will result in gains in operational efficiency.

Weighted Average Cost of Capital (WACC)

Another factor to be considered in an M&A situation is the nature of the relationship between the acquirer and target. If the target company is not in the same industry as the acquirer, then it can be assumed that the target will operate autonomously or as a stand-alone enterprise. In such an instance, the weighted average cost of capital (WACC) of the target company should be used when determining the discount rate for the firm's projected and terminal value. In a case where the target company is to operate autonomously, the risk to the investor is based solely on the risk associated with the target's cash flow.

In many cases, the M&A transaction was based on the potential "synergies" that would occur as a result of a merger. Synergies generally assume that the acquirer and target company are in the same industry and will combine the cash flows of the two organizations. Strategic acquisitions can alter cash flow considerably, and depending upon the perceived value of this variable and others, a "value" placed on potential synergies can have a pronounced affect on the final bid (or premium paid) for a company. Synergies are often a major consideration in negotiations regarding M&A deals. Analysts must take into consideration which WACC (acquirer's or target's) is appropriate for use in discounting combined cash flows. More variables are introduced at this point in the analysis, including risks to cash future cash flow and consideration of the financial structure of the post-merger firm.

In general, if a merger has occurred between two similar industries, the WACC of the acquirer can be used with the assumption that the business risk is similar for both firms. If the target company and acquirer are in different industries, the business risks are inherently different and unique; as are the assets, collateral and debt-paying abilities of each firm. As a rule of thumb, the business and financial risk of a firm should reflect the business of the target company if it is in a different industry than the acquiring firm.

Benefits of the DCF Valuation Method

The following points underscore some of the benefits of using the DCF valuation method (Chaplinsky, 2000):

- Not tied to historical accounting values. Is forward-looking- to future revenue.
- Focuses on cash flow, not profits. Reflects non-cash charges and investment inflows and outflows.
- Separates the investment and financing effects into discrete variables.
- Recognizes the time value of money.
- Allows private information or special insights to be incorporated explicitly.
- Allows expected operating strategy to be incorporated explicitly.
- Embodies the operating costs and benefits of intangible assets.

Conclusion

This paper outlines several different valuation methods that might be used to determine business value. It is generally acknowledged that no valuation method is absolute. "Every number in valuation is measured with error because of flawed methods to describe the past or because of uncertainty about the future" (Chaplinsky, 2000). Different valuation methods may be used for different components of a business and it may be easier to value a division or a product line than an entire company. Another way to use valuation methods is to use different scenarios to test differing results.

It is true that a large portion of the value of any stock or equity in a business comes from the terminal value, but it would be surprising if it were not so. When you buy a stock or invest in the equity of a business, consider how you get your returns. Assuming that your investment is a good investment, the bulk of the returns come not while you hold the equity (from dividends or other cash flows) but when you sell it (from price appreciation). The terminal value is designed to capture the latter. Consequently, the greater the growth potential in a business, the higher the proportion of the value that comes from the terminal value will be (Damodaran, 2002).

Terms & Concepts

Burn Rate (Cash Burn Rate): For a company with negative cash flow, the rate of that negative cash flow, usually per month. Often used by venture capitalists to measure how much time a startup has to reach positive cash flow.

Discounted Cash Flows: A valuation method used to estimate the attractiveness of an investment opportunity. Discounted cash flow (DCF) analysis uses future free cash flow projections and discounts them (most often using the weighted average cost of capital) to arrive at a present value, which is used to evaluate the potential for investment. If the value arrived at through DCF analysis is higher than the current cost of the investment, the opportunity may be a good one.

Multiples: A valuation theory based on the idea that similar assets sell at similar prices. This assumes that a ratio comparing value to some firm-specific variable (operating margins, cash flow, etc.) is the same across similar firms.

Perpetuity: An annuity that has no definite end, or a stream of cash payments that continues forever. Perpetuities are one of the time value of money methods for valuing financial assets.

Steady State (aka Stable Growth): As a firm grows, it will be difficult for it to sustain high growth. Eeventually, the firm will grow at a rate less than or equal to the growth rate of the economy in which it operates.

Synergy: Corporate synergy refers to a financial benefit that a corporation expects to realize when it merges with or acquires another corporation. This type of synergy is a nearly ubiquitous feature of a corporate acquisition and is a negotiating point between the buyer and seller that impacts the final price both parties agree to.

Target Company: A company that is being considered for acquisition.

Terminal Value: In finance, the terminal value of a security is the present value *at a future point in time* of all future cash flows when we expect stable growth rate forever. It is most often used in multi-stage discounted cash flow analysis, and allows for the limitation of cash flow projections to a several-year period.

Time Value of Money: The idea that money available at the present time is worth more than the same amount in the future, due to its potential earning capacity. This core principle of finance holds that, provided money can earn interest, any amount of money is worth more the sooner it is received. Also referred to as "present discounted value."

Weighted Average Cost of Capital (WACC): Broadly speaking, a company's assets are financed by either debt or equity. WACC is the average of the costs of these sources of financing, each of which is weighted by its respective use in the given situation. By taking a weighted average, we can see how much interest the company has to pay for every dollar it finances.

Bibliography

Chaplinsky, S. (2000). Methods of valuation for mergers and acquisitions. Darden Business Publishing. University of Virginia. Retrieved September 20, 2007, from http://www.darden.edu/casecomp/pdf/F-1274.pdf

Damodaran, A. (2002). Closure in valuation: Estimating terminal value. New York University. Retrieved September 18, 2007, from http://pages.stern.nyu.edu/~adamodar/pdfiles/valn2ed/ch12.pdf

Jenkins, D. (2006). The benefits of hybrid valuation models. *CPA Journal, 76*(1), 48-50. Retrieved September 19, 2007, from EBSCO Online Database Business Source Complete. http://search.ebscohost.com/login.aspx?direct=true&db=bth&AN=19365490&site=ehost-live

Giddy, I. (2006). Methods of corporate valuation. *Resources in Finance.* Retrieved September 20, 2007, from http://pages.stern.nyu.edu/~igiddy/valuationmethods.htm

McKee, T. (2004). A new approach to uncertainty in business valuations. *CPA Journal, 74*(4), 46-48. Retrieved September 19, 2007, from EBSCO Online Database Business Source Complete. http://search.ebscohost.com/login.aspx?direct=true&db=bth&AN=12753318&site=ehost-live

Meitner, M. (2013). Multi-period asset lifetimes and accounting-based equity valuation: take care with constant-growth terminal value models!. *Abacus, 49*(3), 340-366. Retrieved November 15, 2013, from EBSCO Online Database Business Source Complete. http://search.ebscohost.com/login.aspx?direct=true&db=bth&AN=90467019&site=ehost-live

Platt, H., Platt, M., & Demirkan, S. (2011). Explaining Stock Price Volatility with Terminal Value Estimates. Journal Of Private Equity, 15(1), 16-25. Retrieved November 15, 2013, from EBSCO Online Database Business Source Complete. http://search.ebscohost.com/login.aspx?direct=true&db=bth&AN=67712913&site=ehost-live

Valuation methodologies. (2005). Met Advisors, Inc. Retrieved September 22, 2007, from http://www.metadvisorsinc.com/Valuation%20Methodologies.pdf

Swad, R. (1994). Discount and capitalization rates in business valuations. *CPA Journal, 69*(10), 40. Retrieved September 19, 2007, from EBSCO Online Database Business Source Complete. http://search.ebscohost.com/login.aspx?direct=true&db=bth&AN=9411292067&site=ehost-live

Yin, C., & Wen, Y. (2013). Optimal dividend problem with a terminal value for spectrally positive Lévy processes. *Insurance: Mathematics & Economics, 53*(3), 769-773. Retrieved November 15, 2013, from EBSCO Online Database Business Source Complete. http://search.ebscohost.com/login.aspx?direct=true&db=bth&AN=92500538&site=ehost-live

Suggested Reading

Courteau, L., Kao, J., & Richardson, G. (2001). Equity valuation employing the ideal versus ad hoc terminal value expressions. *Contemporary Accounting Research, 18*(4), 625-661. Retrieved September 19, 2007, from EBSCO Online Database Business Source Complete. http://search.

ebscohost.com/login.aspx?direct=true&db=bth&AN=6049893&site=ehost-live

DeAngelo, L. (1990). Equity valuation and corporate control. *Accounting Review, 65*(1), 93-112. Retrieved September 19, 2007, from EBSCO Online Database Business Source Complete. http://search.ebscohost.com/login.aspx?direct=true&db=bth&AN=9603274030&site=ehost-live

Penman, S. (2006). Handling valuation models. *Journal of Applied Corporate Finance, 18*(2), 48-55. Retrieved September 19, 2007, from EBSCO Online Database Business Source Complete. http://search.ebscohost.com/login.aspx?direct=true&db=bth&AN=21194447&site=ehost-live

Essay by Carolyn Sprague, MLS

Carolyn Sprague holds a BA degree from the University of New Hampshire and a Masters Degree in Library Science from Simmons College. Carolyn gained valuable business experience as owner of her own restaurant which she operated for 10 years. Since earning her graduate degree Carolyn has worked in numerous library/information settings within the academic, corporate and consulting worlds. Her operational experience as a manger at a global high tech firm and more recent work as a web content researcher have afforded Carolyn insights into many aspects of today's challenging and fast-changing business climate.

Debt Valuation

Table of Contents

Abstract

Overview
- Rising Corporate Debt
- Negative Impacts of Debt

Applications
- Risk Assessment of Debt
- The Value of Debt
- Gross Value
- Growth of Debt
- Debt Management

Issues
- Propping up Companies
- Private Equity
- Pricing Risk

Conclusion

Terms & Concepts

Bibliography

Suggested Reading

Abstract

Debt valuation can be defined as the appraisal of the amount of debt that has been incurred by a company. Companies incur debt or secure credit for a number of reasons that may include the financing of organizational growth, financing a merger or acquisition or to keep an organization solvent during a financial downturn. Some organizations wish to avoid debt at any cost and use the pay-as-you-go strategy to finance growth and operations. Other organizations see debt (or securing credit) as a way to finance growth and opportunities that might otherwise be beyond reach. This essay discusses the implications of business debt from the opportunity standpoint and explores the ways in which debt has been used to fund an era of recent and unprecedented corporate growth and mergers and acquisitions. The rise in the levels of corporate debt will be discussed in terms of its historical significance and the current challenges that organizations face in securing and managing their debt. No current review of this topic would be complete without discussing the role of private equity firms (PE) and the phenomenon of leveraged buyouts (LBO) and their role in the explosion of corporate debt.

Overview

The rise of the issuance of corporate debt from 2003-2007 has been astounding by almost any measure. Low interest rates, rising corporate profits and lots of global credit are cited as helping to fuel an era of rising corporate debt. The early years of the new millennium are somewhat reminiscent of the credit markets that were the norm in the 1990s. In the 1990s, corporate bond issuance or selling of corporate debt was very high. Rapid economic growth was occurring, but the corporate debt load was also bigger than it had ever been. Many felt that even a slight slowing of the economy combined with a rise in interest rates could change manageable debt into debt that would put corporations and individuals under strain. In the 1990s, big debt payments caused companies to cut back on capital expenditures and the potential downturn in the economy was seen as a sure sign that defaults would rise, liquidity would dry up and an overall credit crunch would arise. In the late 1990s, companies were borrowing at rates that had never previously been experienced. Corporate debt was being used for:

- Corporate stock buy-backs (re-purchases)
- Financing for acquisitions and mergers
- Funding of high tech prospects for exponential growth
- Telecom industry growth.

Rising Corporate Debt

The following examples show the trend toward rising corporate debt in the late 1990s. Computer Associates (a high tech darling) had just $50 million in long term debt in 1995, but by 1999, its debt service was $5 billion. Telecom growth was spurred by de-regulation, new technology and competition and debt was incurred by many companies to make a move in the market. During the first half of 1999 alone, $20 billion in corporate defaults had occurred worldwide with 85% being in the USA.

The following warning was being sounded in late 1999. "The most alarming sign of trouble ahead may be what's happening to corporate balance sheets. Despite the huge gains in the stock market, there is a pronounced tilt in corporate financing toward debt and away from equity. Even at today's prices, companies are buying back far more stock than they are issuing. Over the past 12 months, an eye-popping 3.6% of gross domestic product went into stock buybacks, and even with the IPO boom, nearly $500 billion in equities have been taken off the market since 1997" (Mandel, 1999).

Negative Impacts of Debt

The dotcom bust of early 2000 was a wakeup call to many investors and financial institutions. Stock prices fell 40%. The Federal Reserve lowered interest rates to help stimulate the economy as threats of recession loomed. Stock prices remained stagnant, but corporate profits kept rising. Many saw the rise of private equity (PE) firms as an natural outcome to economic conditions shortly after the tech/telecom bust. Those conditions were: Depressed stock prices, low interest rates and rising corporate profits. With a "dollop" of cash and loads of debt, PE firms began to snap up companies on the cheap. The average buyout in 2002 was 4 times the price of the company's cash flow (aka EBITA). It was not uncommon for PE firms to borrow 70% of the purchase price for these acquisitions. The loans were then put on the acquired company's balance sheet which doubled or even tripled the company's debt load (Tully & Hajim, 2007).

By 2003, the Federal Reserve had slashed interest rates in an effort to get the economy growing after the tech/telecom bust. Corporate profits continued to remain strong, and with the opening of global markets and associated global credit, the era of corporate mergers was ushered in. Lots of cheap and readily available credit and a higher tolerance for risk helped bolster many private equity firms and their LBO deals.

A brief discussion of differing attitudes about the value of debt will follow as well as an overview of corporate credit ratings as they pertain to today's trends in corporate debt. Finally, this essay will outline some of the current trends and outlooks related to tightening credit markets, investor risk tolerance and the potential for market corrections in relation to potential corporate failure.

Applications

Risk Assessment of Debt

Corporate credit ratings help investors determine the amount of risk associated with acquiring debt. Credit ratings are independent objective assessments of credit worthiness. Ratings "measure the ability or willingness of an entity (person or company) to keep its financial commitment to repay debt obligations (Heakal, 2003). Three of the most widely respected raters of corporate credit are: Moody's, Standard & Poor's, and Fitch IBCA. Each of these rating agencies provides a rating system that helps to determine the credit risk when acquiring a corporation's debt. Ratings can be assigned to long term or short term debt. For example, Standard and Poor's AAA rating is given to companies with the highest investment grade and very low credit risk. This credit-worthiness indicated a company's high ability and willingness to repay its debt. "Investment grade" is the level of quality that is generally thought to be required for an investor considering overseas investments. It is interesting to note that in the 1990s, investment grade was more of a requisite for incurring debt than it has been in recent years. PE firms have not paid as much attention to the ratings (since 2003) and have basically been much more tolerant of risk as many PE firms have bought and sold lower grade or "junk" investments.

Chart 1: An Overview of Moody's and Standard & Poor's ratings

Bond Ratings			
Moody's	Standard & Poor's	Grade	Risk
Aaa	AAA	Investment	Lowest Risk
Aa	AA	Investment	Low Risk
A	A	Investment	Low Risk
Baa	BBB	Investment	Medium Risk
Ba, B	BB, B	Junk	High Risk
Caa/Ca/C	CCC/CC/C	Junk	Highest Risk
C	D	Junk	In Default

The Value of Debt

Many companies are opposed to borrowing funds or leveraging debt to fund operations and growth. Many privately-held companies are debt-free by choice, while many other companies (ex: service companies) don't have the means to support long-term borrowing and are debt-free by necessity. Many business owners and corporate management teams feel a great deal of security in knowing that their organizations are not mired in debt, and may even have a sense that a lack of debt makes their business more attractive in the marketplace. However, in the age of global markets and virtual customers in a "flat world" economy, many see debt as a strategic tool to be leveraged to support growth.

Gross Value

Having some debt on the books may be a selling point when it comes to the overall "gross value" of an organization. Gross value, to many, includes what a company earns, but also may reflect its value or brand in the marketplace. Intangible assets can be leveraged by companies who expand their market reach and presence in global markets. Sophisticated buyers or investors will look at overall capital structure. Debt is necessary for many organizations to invest in growth and gain increased market share. Lack of debt may indicate a non-aggressive stance in the marketplace; global brands can't afford to shy away from opportunity that might hinder growth. From a growth and expansion view, corporate debt can be seen a very positive thing. However, investors would be well advised to avoid debt that is not necessary, overly costly or of high risk (Fraser, 2000).

Growth of Debt

The amount of debt that is on many company's balance sheets went from reasonable to outrageous between 2003 and 2007. Debt, once thought of as a necessary evil to help companies finance growth and expansion, became the hottest investment opportunity of the early 21st century.

"Like every mania, this one carried the seeds of its own destruction. The lure of easy riches drew new players, and the pace of deal making picked up. In 2005 there was a string of splendid deals at reasonable prices. As the good times rolled, the buyout binge took on a life of its own. The real craziness started in 2006. Dazzled by rich returns, investors threw more and more money at private equity firms. Flush with cash, the PE shops started pushing prices to unsustainable heights" (Tully & Hajim, 2007, ¶10).

Debt Management

In 2007, the economy slid into recession and bad debt began to have serious repercussions worldwide. Shudders in financial markets surrounding sub-prime mortgage troubles shouldn't have affected most holders of corporate debt, but many saw the tightening of global credit as inevitable. The cycle headed down from its heady high, and there was renewed pressure on management teams at public companies to manage debt; private equity was not be able to "bail out" troubled companies, notably General Motors, and the federal government stepped in with taxpayer money to prevent the collapse of institutions considered "too big to fail." Credit became scarce, even after the federal reserve lowered interest rates to near zero to stimulate lending. Lenders are not likely to return to the liberal lending policies of the early 2000s (Shearer, 2007).

The media is full of sound bites that warn investors that much of what happens in the stock market is cyclical ("Spreading caution," 2007).

Issues

Propping up Companies

"Low interest rates and a flood of cash have helped many troubled companies skirt certain demise in recent years, which has led to an era of record low defaults and put a strain on the entire sector" (Kirby, 2007, ¶4). According to Alex Jurshevski, CEO of Recovery Partners in Toronto, "'The whole industry has been depressed because of the default rate,' says Jurshevski. who, despite having $500 million at his disposal, has yet to put any of it to work. Now, as the sub-prime mortgage collapse sends ripples beyond the housing sector, some foresee a credit crunch spreading to other sectors. 'I hope so,' he says. 'All the bad loans have already been made. They're just waiting to turn bad, like fruit left out on the counter'" (Kirby, 2007, ¶4).

During the global financial crisis of 2008, central banks around the world pumped hundreds of billions of dollars in cash into financial markets to stave off a crisis. Yet failure is an integral part of the business cycle. "If you don't have a cleansing process where certain firms go under, the pain is delayed. Generally that means the pain will be that much greater later on" (Kirby, 2007).

"Defaults, which are triggered when companies fail to make debt repayments or break the terms of their loan contracts, have hovered around zero for the last three years. In a typical year, default rates on corporate loans and bonds can be anywhere from 3% to 10% or even higher. Even the riskiest of loans have handily dodged insolvency until now. That's because companies struggling with their debt have found a steady stream of investment funds willing to give them ever more money. 'On the one hand nobody is going bankrupt and nobody's getting thrown out of work,' says Jurshevski. 'But it also means there may be a lot of people lending money on non-economic terms and that means firms that shouldn't be surviving are being kept afloat by cheap credit.' Investors are worried buyers won't be able to handle their debt loads if interest rates rise further" (Kirby, 2007, ¶7).

Private Equity

Between 2006 and 2008, there was huge activity in the high yield and leverage loan market. Sub investment grade ratings loans raised $146 trillion in 257 deals and $950 billion in 2219 leveraged loan deals. The increase in transactions is attributed to an increase in debt-raising by private equity firms which are used to fund buyouts. Blackstone Group, a private equity firm, financed 75-80% of its deal through debt. Blackstone has acted as a buyer, a broker w/other firms that it owns and as a lender. Blackstone has had huge success in its deals — many attribute Blackstone's success to a core of talented partners with industry and financial expertise. Because Blackstone partners have vertical and sector depth of knowledge, "they have the wherewithal to dig deep when doing transactions and figure out the most flexible and cost-efficient capital structures to match the investment needs of the businesses they are buying. This has paid off regarding their ability to handle complex transactions" ("Blackstone group," 2007; Segal, 2013).

Some think the level of debt of private equity firms is too high and that the same firms may not be informing investors of the true level of risk when they buy debt. Some high profile LBO deals have happened in industries that investors would normally shy away from. However, firms like Blackstone have gained a huge amount of trust in the debt business. There's an underlying fear that liquidity will dry up and private equity firms will get left holding debt that they won't easily be able to dispose of. Many LBOs are actually completed with unfavorable credit terms and then are renegotiated with financial institutions at a better rate. A firm like Blackstone has capitalized on the debt business and has gained the confidence of investment bankers who trust firms like Blackstone that are experts in debt ("Blackstone group," 2007).

Pricing Risk

Firm failure is a natural part of the business cycle. However, it has been a rare part of the cycle since 2003 and is likely due to a couple of factors. After the collapse of the tech bubble around 2000, the Federal Reserve slashed interest rates. Low interest rates and increased global liquidity that was raised by hedge funds and private equity firms produced tons of cash in global markets. Businesses took advantage of the cheap cash by borrowing heavily to fund acquisitions and expansions. The rate of defaults on loans and business failures has been very low to almost non-existent during this period. Defaults result from a failure of a company to repay its debt, or when a company fails to honor the terms of a loan contract.

Many contend that money was so cheap and easy to come by that even firms that should have gone under found a steady flow of cash to keep them solvent. Banks ceased operating on a "slash and burn" or "close-the-door liquidations" policy as they once did. Lenders are looking for alternatives to foreclosures and defaults and usually reserve those scenarios for firms that are responsible for fraudulent business practices or gross mismanagement. In mid 2007, there were a few high profile examples where private equity firms had trouble selling corporate debt. While these examples are still relatively rare, concern lingered that some small and medium firms could have also fall into debt trouble.

Risk for some firms means opportunity for others — there are companies that will benefit from a rise in the corporate default on loans. Miscalculations on the risk/reward equation will cost some companies their very existence and many investors acknowledge that this is a necessary part of the business cycle. Central banks have been accused of pumping billions into financial markets to stave off corporate collapse (some of which should be allowed to happen). Recovery Partners, a Toronto based company, is in just that market. Recovery Partners has cash in hand for the sole purpose of buying portfolios of underperforming corporations. According to Alex Jurshevski, "By snatching up the debt of struggling companies, he aims to take over the businesses, turn their fortunes around, and resell them. It's a precarious strategy, akin, he says, to safely catching a falling knife, but it's one that promises huge returns" (Kirby, 2007).

Conclusion

Private equity firms were blamed for creating a "market that is completely out of touch with economic reality." Private equity has been called the perfect Wall Street bubble for its part in making fortunes from increasingly risky investments and strategies. Predictions of tightening of credit markets came true, while optimism that robust global markets would provide investors with corporate debt as well as investment capital fell far short, at least for a time. The financial crisis of 2008 was accompanied by a credit drought and worldwide contraction and was followed by a glacial recovery.

Putting corporate debt on a company's balance sheet can provide necessary capital from investors to fund expansion or acquisition. Reasonable amounts of investment grade debt are the safest bet for companies to incur. In 2002 the average buy-out of a company was four times its cash flow; in 2007 buyout prices were closing at 15 times cash flow-or 4 times the rate of 2002 (Tully & Hajim, 2007). By 2012, as the economy began to show signs of recovery from the worst downturn since the Great Depression, private equity firms were once again able to borrow the lion's share of funds toward a leveraged buyout — at a very low interest rate — if the target companies were stable, had tangible assets, and maintained a healthy cash flow (Sheahan, 2012).

Terms & Concepts

Corporate Debt: Short or long term debt issued as securities by corporations. Short term debt is issued as commercial paper. Long term debt is issued as bonds/notes.

Corporate Credit Rating: Corporate credit ratings are assigned by credit rating agencies (for example Standard & Poor's) and are designated by letter groupings (for example AAA, B, or CC). These ratings serve as finance indicators to potential debt securities investors.

Credit Crunch: A shortage of available loans. This could raise interest rates, but it usually means that certain borrowers are unable to get loans due to credit rationing.

Debt Security: A security that represents a loan given to an issuer by an investor. In exchange for the loan the issuer makes a commitment to pay interest and completely repay the debt on a predetermined date.

EBITA: Earnings before interest, taxes, depreciation, and amortization.

High Yield Debt: A bond rated lower than investment grade when it is purchased. These bonds are riskier in situations of default or adverse credit but usually yield higher returns than higher quality bonds to entice investors.

Leveraged Recapitalization: A technique employed to avoid involuntary acquisition. Using this strategy, a company takes on a significant amount of debt in order to repurchase stocks through a buyback offer or dispenses a significant dividend between current shareholders. The company share price then increases significantly, which makes the company less appealing as a takeover target.

Mezzanine Loan: Mezzanine loans can be compared to second mortgages, apart from the fact that a mezzanine loan is secured by company stock of the company owning the property rather than by the real estate property itself.

Private Equity Firms: Any type of non-public Ownership Equity security not listed on the public exchange. An investor who wants to sell private equity securities must find a buyer without the help of a public marketplace. There are three ways in which private equity firms usually obtain returns on their investments: An IPO, a sale or merger of the company they own, or a recapitalization.

Risk Assessment: A technique used to measure two different quantities of risk: The size of the possible loss and the likelihood of the loss occurring.

Sub-investment Grade Loans: Also referred to as junk bonds, or high yield bonds, they are issued by companies carrying an uncertain credit rating. Any credit rating lower than "BBB" is considered to be an uncertain, or speculative, grade.

Bibliography

Beware of the debt bomb. (1999, November 1). *Business Week*, (3653), 220. Retrieved September 17, 2007, from EBSCO Online Database Academic Search Premier. http://search.ebscohost.com/login.aspx?direct=true&db=aph&AN=2410703&site=ehost-live

Blackstone group. (2007). *Euromoney, 38*(458), 100. Retrieved September 14, 2007, from EBSCO Online Database Business Source Premier. http://search.ebscohost.com/login.aspx?direct=true&db=buh&AN=25585141&site=ehost-live

Corporate finance. (2007). *QuickMBA.com.* Retrieved September 14, 2007, from http://www.quickmba.com/finance/cf/

Frasier, J. (2000) Giving credit to debt. *Inc.com: The Daily Resource for Entrepreneurs.*. Retrieved September 15, 2007, from http://www.inc.com/magazine/20001101/20913.html

Kirby, J. (2007). Let the feasting begin. *Maclean's, 120*(33), 30-31. Retrieved September 14, 2007, from EBSCO Online Database Academic Search Premier. http://search.ebscohost.com/login.aspx?direct=true&db=aph&AN=26295581&site=ehost-live

Heakal, R. (2003). What is a corporate credit rating? *Investopedia.* Retrieved September 14, 2007, from http://www.investopedia.com/articles/03/102203.asp

Mandel, M. (1999, November 1). Is the U.S. building a debt bomb? *Business Week*, (3653), 40-42. Retrieved September 17, 2007, from EBSCO Online Database Academic Search Premier. http://search.ebscohost.com/login.aspx?direct=true&db=aph&AN=2409107&site=ehost-live

Rosenbush, S. (2007, July 30). Corporate debt: Dressed up, nowhere to go. *Business Week Online*, 11. Retrieved September 14, 2007, from EBSCO Online Database Academic Search Premier. http://search.ebscohost.com/login.aspx?direct=true&db=aph&AN=26003795&site=ehost-live

Segal, J. (2013). Blackstone Group's GSO Capital: lenders of last resort. *Institutional Investor, 47*(6), 12. Retrieved November 15, 2013, from EBSCO Online Database Business Source Complete. http://search.ebscohost.com/login.aspx?direct=true&db=bth&AN=90371235&site=ehost-live

Sheahan, M. (2012). Private equity firms writing smaller checks. *High Yield Report, 23*(21), 23. Retrieved November 15, 2013, from EBSCO Online Database Business Source Complete. http://search.ebscohost.com/login.aspx?direct=true&db=bth&AN=75649108&site=ehost-live

Shearer, B. (2007). Deal market braces for credit crunch. *Mergers & Acquisitions: The Dealermaker's Journal, 42*(9), 74-91. Retrieved September 14, 2007, from EBSCO Online Database Business Source Premier. http://search.ebscohost.com/login.aspx?direct=true&db=buh&AN=26484343&site=ehost-live

Spreading caution. (2007). *Economist, 384*(8539), 76. Retrieved September 14, 2007, from EBSCO Online Database Academic Search Premier. http://search.ebscohost.com/login.aspx?direct=true&db=aph&AN=25952117&site=ehost-live

Tully, S., & Hajim, C. (2007). Why the private equity bubble is bursting. *Fortune, 156*(4), 30-34. Retrieved September 14, 2007, from EBSCO Online Database Academic Search Premier. http://search.ebscohost.com/login.aspx?direct=true&db=aph&AN=26199030&site=ehost-live

Suggested Reading

Clouse, C. (2007). Mounting debt may spell opportunity for some investment banks. *Private Placement Letter, 25*(31), 1-6. Retrieved September 14, 2007, from EBSCO Online Database Business Source Premier. http://search.ebscohost.com/login.aspx?direct=true&db=buh&AN=26096492&site=ehost-live

Karp, A. (2006). Cash crunch. *Air Cargo World, 96*(2), 10-11. Retrieved September 14, 2007, from EBSCO Online Database Business Source Premier. http://search.ebscohost.com/login.aspx?direct=true&db=buh&AN=19819894&site=ehost-live

S., M. (2007). Distressed debt outlook: Make room for a little doom and gloom. *Bank Loan Report, 22*(2), 5. Retrieved September 14, 2007, from EBSCO Online Database Business Source Premier. http://search.ebscohost.com/login.aspx?direct=true&db=buh&AN=23768870&site=ehost-live

Woyke, E., & Henry, D. (2007, August 13). The buyout boom's dark side. *Business Week*, (4046), 40-42. Retrieved September 14, 2007, from EBSCO Online Database Academic Search Premier. http://search.ebscohost.com/login.aspx?direct=true&db=aph&AN=26057452&site=ehost-live

---

Essay by Carolyn Sprague, MLS

Carolyn Sprague holds a BA degree from the University of New Hampshire and a Masters Degree in Library Science from Simmons College. Carolyn gained valuable business experience as owner of her own restaurant which she operated for 10 years. Since earning her graduate degree Carolyn has worked in numerous library/information settings within the academic, corporate and consulting worlds. Her operational experience as a manger at a global high tech firm and more recent work as a web content researcher have afforded Carolyn insights into many aspects of today's challenging and fast-changing business climate.

Warrants & Convertibles

Table of Contents

Abstract
Overview
　Historical Perspective on Investing
Applications
　Investment Vehicles
　Warrants
　Convertible Securities
Conclusion
Terms & Concepts
Bibliography
Suggested Reading

Abstract

This article begins with a brief history and an overview of financial investment vehicles, providing insight from the corporate as well as the investor's perspective. The reader is offered a detailed description of warrant certificates and convertible bonds, underscored with the benefits and disadvantages of each. The circumstances under which warrants or convertibles are issued by companies as a financial vehicle for investors, as opposed to common or other types of stocks or bonds is made apparent, offering valuable perspective to potential investors or issuers of these vehicles. The role of the Securities and Exchange Commission (SEC) in governance and oversight of companies' security offerings is not insubstantial and a brief high-level mention is delivered in this review.

Overview

Historical Perspective on Investing

In 1792, the first organized stock exchange was transacted in New York. Financial leaders at the time developed and agreed to a formal document of rules, regulations and fees for trading stocks and bonds; hence the launch of the stock market phenomenon. In simpler times, securities were auctioned off to the highest bidder, with the seller paying a commission on each stock sold. History holds lessons for the experienced, in terms of investments and risk, highlighted in the rapid growth in the stock market and in investors' frenetic drive to swift profits.

In addition to investors' entrepreneurial drive, interest in the common good has played a vital role in the world of stocks, bonds and investments. Soon after the United States became involved in World War II, it became paramount to enhance the efficiency and safety of existing rail transport systems. Success in the wartime endeavor hinged upon accessibility and mobility for people and resources. The railroad system at the time was woefully inadequate in terms of financing, which subsequently disadvantaged the rail's ability to meet demand.

The Interstate Commerce Act of 1887 was responsible for having created the Interstate Commerce Commission, which, under great influence from private farmers and others, prohibited the railroads from increasing rates sufficient to meet growing operating costs. Compounding the cash scarcity, the strict regulations most certainly prevented the rail from creating a positive financial margin with which to make needed capital investments in the company. Put simply, the railroads, a key element in our nation's transportation infrastructure, simply could not support growth or sustain operations without investors and their cash. The railroads ultimately were built with money from men who hoped to earn a large profit from their investment in operations and capital.

In context, today's large corporations with vast numbers of stockholders still rely on investors' interest to grow, much as the railroads offered a financial interest and a public service to the country during a critical time of conflict. The story of economics has always been influenced by enlarging corporations, in particular those representing importance to the public at large. Commodities, such as oil, wheat, corn and soybeans, are a modern day example of investments of great public import and guaranteed financial growth. The rail of yesterday, given its history, might well have been considered a primary commodity of its time.

Applications

Investment Vehicles

Companies can offer investors numerous venues in which to place their financial interests and test their financial expertise, no matter their level of experience. Corporations may finance part of their business by leveraging themselves with securities they promise to pay back, with interest, in addition to the principle. Variations on this model will be introduced later in this essay. The more debt the company incurs, naturally, the higher the organization's financial risk. A few examples of investment vehicles utilized by corporations and the government to support their financial needs include:

- Convertibles;
- Corporate, municipal, or treasury bonds;
- Common Stock;
- Commodities markets;
- Governmental, corporate and municipal bonds;
- Warrant certificates.

Warrants

Common stock warrants offer the investor the right to buy common stock at a specific price, in the future, within a set period of time. In some cases, warrants have no expiration date; these are known as perpetual warrants. If one were looking to identify warrants on the stock listing, he or she would look for the suffix "wt." An installment warrant is an option that offers a share on credit; with the installment vehicle, the investor pays for half the share now and for the rest later. The initial installment provides the owner half a stock. The premise behind installment warrants is that they represent a long term call option (opportunity to exercise a warrant when stock price exceeds the initial investment price, resulting in a net profit) for investors who are inclined to speculate that the price of stock will increase in the long term; the longer the life before the warrant's expiration, the higher its value and the safer the investor's money. The anticipation for the investor is that the company will see increased profits in its future years, thereby growing its dividends. The owner of the warrant can watch and speculate (within the context of the expiration date) until such time as the stock and dividends look attractive enough to 'exercise' or turn the warrant over to stock ownership.

It is evident that investors should educate themselves thoroughly in the warrant vehicle and the issuing company before making this somewhat speculative investment; this education includes attention to transaction costs which will impact profit and loss calculations. "ABN AMRO's {a global banking group) Aaron Stambulich notes that while installments offer a lower-risk form of leverage than other forms of equity lending, investors still need to spend the time acquiring the knowledge to use them properly,'" (Walker, 2007).

Shorter term warrants do exist; they represent a higher risk with a robust appeal of higher returns to the investor. Both long and short-term warrants are priced lower than the common stock purchase price, thereby creating leverage and risk to the corporation, similar to bond arrangements (bonds are in essence a loan with interest). Warrants, however, do not earn interest and usually have an expiration date which can vary depending on the model employed; the key point is that warrants become worthless at expiration date or when the cost of common stock drops to a very low rate. Warrants offer no dividends or voting rights to the warrant owner. "{Warrants} are derivatives — this means they derive their value from and give investors exposure to an underlying asset, such as a share, basket of shares, index, currency or commodity, at a fraction of the underlying asset's cost (Walker, 2007).

Valuation of the Warrant

The value of the warrant is the price of the company's common stock minus the warrant's option price. As a simple example, if the price of the warrant certificate is $15 and the common stock purchase price is $20, the warrant is worth $5. In contrast, if the warrant certificate price is $20 and the stock price is $15, the warrant holds no value. It will remain so unless the stock price, in this case, enjoys favorable appreciation to bring its value above the warrant price. The higher the common stock's price, obviously, the greater the warrant's value. If the common stock is volatile, all the better for the warrant owner, as this too increases the value of the warrant.

When a warrant certificate is exercised (turned over for stock ownership) the number of shares in the company increases and the stock price does decrease overall. If there are warrants outstanding, the owners of the stock are obligated to satisfy the call (exercising) from warrant holders. The money paid to purchase the warrant at the outset goes directly to the company as does the money paid when the owner exercises the warrant to purchase common stock. The new shares generated through an exercised warrant are accounted for in financial reports as *fully diluted earnings per share*, which represents what the earnings per share would be if all warrants were exercised and all outstanding convertible securities, were converted to stock. In essence, the denominator (total outstanding shares) increases, so the value of earnings per share dips lower.

Warrants are sometimes attached to bonds or preferred stock as a means to reduce the interest or the dividends that have to be paid to sell the securities. These particular warrants, issued in this bundled format can be separated and traded independently of the bond or stock and are termed detachable warrants.

Warrants as Stock Options

In today's highly competitive environment, companies struggle to attract a strong, talented workforce. Stock options, sometimes offered as an enticement to potential employees, are commonly issued by companies in the form of a warrant. Start-up companies will offer the stock option as an alternative or adjunct to salary, in order to minimize cash expenditures, while creating an attractive option for recruitment purposes. The disadvantage of warrant stock options, if exercised, is that it decreases the value of the existing shareholders' stock, as referenced earlier in this essay.

Public Accounting & the Securities and Exchange Commission (SEC)

When a warrant is exercised (converted to stock), although it means more funds for the company, the company's balance sheet has historically retained the debt.

"Issuers ordinarily expect to account for common stock and warrants as equity, and account for debt as liabilities" (Dyson, 2007). The Financial Accounting Standards Board (FASB) and the Securities and Exchange Commission (SEC) recognize that for issuers there may be inconsistency and misinterpretation on how warrants and convertibles are reported on the books. The SEC has required registrants {of the SEC} to restate their financial statements to reflect its current interpretation of the existing literature (Dyson, 2007). Companies' first step is to identify whether they fall under the scope of the FASB's SFAS 150 which lists the various features of securities placing the instrument as a liability as opposed to an asset. The author of *Freestanding Warrants and Embedded Conversion Options*, Robert A. Dyson, cautions as follows:

> "In recent years the accounting for detachable warrants and convertible securities has grown more complex. The increased SEC interest and constantly evolving rules have created much risk for both preparers and auditors of financial statements. The incorrect application of EITF 00-19 has resulted in financial statement restatement reflecting the reclassification of equity instruments to liabilities and changes of fair value of those liabilities as charges to earnings" (Dyson, 2007).

It is not within the scope of this essay to provide financial accounting direction, rather to provide to the business reader highlights of important issues and an awareness of corporate obligations. Identifying regulatory applications and staying abreast of constantly changing directives and definitions is a key to the success of any executive whose business is involved with sales or investment in financial vehicles.

Convertible Securities

There are two types of convertible securities addressed in this essay: First is the convertible bond and the second is convertible preferred stock.

- First, the convertible bond is, by definition, issued by a corporation, and not by the government. A convertible bond is nothing more than an arrangement whereby the bond can be converted into specific predetermined numbers of common stock in the company, should the bondholder exercise the option. A conversion price is identified so as to make the security attractive when the stock price increases substantially. The value of the bond is not an exact science, but represents the estimate of the value of common stock in the company at the time of its issuance, as if there were no conversion options. The conversion ratio dictates how many shares into which the convertible bond can be converted.

- Preferred stock convertibles provide for conversion of the security to preferred stock, which is a favorable class of ownership in which the investors' dividends are paid out before common stock dividends are. Preferred stock owners generally do not have voting rights, unlike common stockholders. The preferred stock is attractive to some investors because it offers fixed dividends as well as appreciation in shares (e.g. equity) in the company.

Convertibles are more attractive to the issuing company than are other types of bonds, because the interest paid on the convertible is lower. A second attractive feature of the convertible bond to the issuing corporation is that it does not, like a warrant, issue new stocks to shareholders or dilute existing stock value. The formula used to transition preferred convertibles to common stock generally includes an anti-dilution provision, of particular import to owners. Similar to warrants, convertibles are attractive to investors who have reason or hope to believe that the company's ultimate stock value will go up. The investor, of course, should be well informed about the company into which he or she is investing money; the value of research, knowing the market and experience cannot be overstated. Companies issuing convertibles tend to be the more speculative ventures on the whole and should alert the investor to watch for risk as well as opportunity.

Advantages of Convertibles

Advantages of convertibles, to the investor, include their tendency not to dip as greatly in value in a Bear Market (a downturn and devaluation in the market) as do common stocks. Should the company go into default (inability to pay), convertibles can be transitioned safely to a bond or preferred stock. In purchasing convertible securities, the investor enjoys the safety of a bond yet is offered the opportunity for value appreciation. Another very attractive feature of convertibles is that they may be purchased through tax-deferred retirement accounts. This represents an opportunity which swings some investors readily to this option.

Disadvantages of Convertibles

Disadvantages of convertible securities include the expectation that they yield less than the common shares or a bond issued by the corporation. Investors should take heed that companies issuing convertibles are often those facing a financially challenging situation, and may be issuing convertible securities as a last chance option for garnering monies for financing. Another disadvantage of convertibles is that the issuing companies may also call the bond, forcing conversion to common stock at a convenient time for the issuer, which may not be a favorable time for the investor to convert. If the common stock price reaches a specified ratio, the issuer is permitted to force conversion before the end before the end of the normal protection period.

Case Study — Ford Motor Company

Ford Motor Company, facing substantial losses in its North American market, and facing near-term liquidity issues, announced plans in late 2006 to raise $18 million to restructure its operations, $3 million of which will be sold in the form of convertibles, which would be converted to Ford Common Stock. A company the size of Ford entering such a high yield market for the first time has raised some eyebrows. Shelley Lombard, senior high yield analyst for the New York company, *Gimme Credit,* states, "The fact that this issuer has not been in the high yield market before and that this company is a very troubled company is what makes this significant" (S., M., & S., G., 2006). Matt Eagan, a portfolio manager with the Boston-based company, Loomis and Sayles states, "Market demand is high and hedge funds will be hungry for Ford's bonds, particularly if they are convertible bonds. If they do end up issuing a convertible bond, we see that there's a lot of demand in that space" (S., M., & S., G., 2006). It is predicted that this unusual offering from Ford could be precedent-setting if successful in growing the companies' capital. Other large corporations will take notice and possibly follow suit.

Case Study — In the Throes of Financial Difficulty for Luminent

Luminent Mortgage Capital, Incorporated, has defaulted on a $90 million debt and is facing even more financial difficulties. Issuing of warrants as an investment vehicle, with the assistance of Arco Capital Corporation will occur in an effort to preserve the financial survival of the company. *American Banker* reports: "Arco Capital Corp. Ltd. of San Juan, Puerto Rico, has agreed to provide up to $125 million of financing to {Luminent Mortgage Capital Inc}, a San Francisco real estate investment trust (Hochstein, 2007). "In return", Luminent said Monday, "Arco has received warrants to buy a 49% voting stake and a 51% "economic interest" in the REIT at an exercise price of 18 cents a share. The warrants are good for five years beginning Aug. 30" (Hochstein, 2007).

Luminent acknowledged "the possibility of sizeable dilution to existing ... stockholders" as a result of the issuance of warrants" (Hochstein, 2007). However, it also said the board's audit committee, "pursuant to an exception provided in the New York Stock Exchange's stockholder approval policy, expressly approved the decision not to seek stockholder approval for the issuance. The committee did so because delays in securing such approval "could, given the external climate, seriously further jeopardize the financial viability of Luminent" (Hochstein, 2007).

Case Study — Good News for Mirant Warrant Holders

"With the $45 billion buy out of TXU {a Dallas based energy company} looming in the smokestacks, chatter of a possible Mirant deal has intensified, bringing to light what is arguably the best play on the utility — its warrants. Should Mirant, an international electricity and producer and seller be acquired for $41 per share, as some analysts estimate, warrant holders will realize a 22% gain, while holders of common stocks will gain 10%. The warrants were purposely developed to protect their owners in case of a cash takeover," (Louria, 2007). For warrant holders, this is good news because specific features were built into the warrants which will very possibly create a windfall for them, contrary to usual happenings in cash takeovers. Until recently, protective features on warrants were not common; but in today's environment of rapid company buy-outs, investors are well-advised to be alert to the availability of such safeguards.

Case Study — Competition for a Warrant offered by Money Magazine

In a well-received competition just this year (2007), warrants were offered to the readers of *Money* who could most closely predict the price of commodities; oil in particular. The response was "A wave of Money readers {trying} to estimate the price of oil a couple of months ahead — a keen investor from Canberra is the winner," (Field, 2007). Commodities have become an attractive vehicle to investors because of the wide global demand for oil as well as growing international tensions with oil-rich countries; these tensions are likely to drive the cost of oil even further. Anyone driving a motorized automobile today is acutely aware of the impact of cost increases in oil. Warrants were offered as a desirable investment vehicle; the response clearly supported the growing attraction of this option. "Part of the appeal of commodity warrants lies in the leverage they offer. Warrants require a far smaller investment than the underlying futures contracts, and the percentage returns can be very high. Investors in commodity warrants certainly don't have to wait long to know if they have made or lost money. For the record commodity warrants issued by CWA (Commodity Warrants Australia) have an average term of 92 days though the average time to maximum profit is just 16 days. CWA says, between August 2005 and February 2007 — a period during which demand for commodities has boomed — around 65% of CWA's commodity warrants generated a positive result, with the average return being 38.4% (Field, 2007).

Conclusion

Knowledge is power, and loaning, buying or selling in the financial market should be approached with much thoughtful preparation. Smaller investors may unwittingly put their trust in an advisor, thinking their investment is safer with what he or she thinks may be an expert in the field. Investment costs and financial risks should be of paramount import to the investor, who is closely monitoring the market for attractive opportunities which provide sufficient safety to meet the investor's comfort level.

Companies, accountable to shareholders or stockholders, rely on their historical performance and their projections for success in the future. Wise resource management, accountability and attention to the SEC guidelines, current and future, are the responsibility of the company attracting the investor. This essay has given a broad overview only and has hopefully enlightened investors and issuers alike to the vast risks and opportunities available in the exciting work of financial markets.

Terms & Concepts

Bear Market: A prolonged period in which investment prices fall, a time of accompanied by extensive doubt and distrust in the market.

Bonds: A debt security, essentially a loan for which the issuer owes the holders a debt, and is obliged to repay both principal and interest of the debt at maturity date.

Call: A contract that gives the holder the right to purchase a given stock at a specific price within a designated period of time.

Commodities: A term for products of value, for which there is demand. The resources are produced in large quantities by many different producers; the items from each are considered comparable — some examples include oil, soybeans, and pork bellies)

EITF-00-19: 'Emerging Issues Task Force '- formed in 1984 in response to the recommendations of the FASB's task force on timely financial reporting guidance; available for public viewing. (http://www.fasb.org/eitf/about%5feitf.shtml).

FASB (Financial Accounting Standards Board): The designated United States (private sector) organization that establishes financial accounting and reporting standards

Investment Vehicle: Broad term defining any method by which money can be invested

Preferred Stock: Preferred stock is typically a higher grade stock than common stock, allowing for dividends to be paid out to the investor before payout to common stock holders.

Puts: An option that allows the holder to sell a given stock at a specific price within a designated period of time.

Securities and Exchange Commission: A U.S. Federal Agency responsible for enforcing the federal securities laws and regulating the stock market and securities industry (stocks, bonds, etc).

Stocks Option: An employee stock option is a call option (see "call' above) on the common stock of a company, representing a non-cash compensation for the employee, an incentive to participate in the company's success.

Bibliography

Dyson, R. (2007). Freestanding warrants and embedded conversion options. *CPA Journal, 77*(4), 40-49. Retrieved September 15, 2007, from EBSCO Online Database Business Source Premier. http://search.ebscohost.com/login.aspx?direct=true&db=buh&AN=24729316&site=ehost-live

Field, N. (2007). Warrants winners. *Money (14446219)*, (92), 94-95. Retrieved September 17, 2007, from EBSCO Online Database Business Source Premier. http://search.ebscohost.com/login.aspx?direct=true&db=buh&AN=25890115&site=ehost-live

Kim, W., Kim, W., & Kim, H. (2013). Death spiral issues in emerging market: A control related perspective. *Pacific-Basin Finance Journal,* 2214-36. Retrieved November 15, 2013, from EBSCO Online Database Business Source Complete. http://search.ebscohost.com/login.aspx?direct=true&db=bth&AN=85174023&site=ehost-live

Louria, A. (2007). Hoping for a warrant windfall. *Investment Dealers' Digest, 73*(9), 9-14. Retrieved September 16, 2007, from EBSCO Online Database Business Source Premier. http://search.ebscohost.com/login.aspx?direct=true&db=buh&AN=24341643&site=ehost-live

S., M., & S., G. (2006). Ford may jump start with new convertible bond. *High Yield Report, 17*(46), 1-8. Retrieved September 16, 2007, from EBSCO Online Database Business Source Premier. http://search.ebscohost.com/login.aspx?direct=true&db=buh&AN=23305561&site=ehost-live

Schwienbacher, A. (2013). The entrepreneur's investor choice: The impact on later-stage firm development. *Journal of Business Venturing, 28*(4), 528-545. Retrieved November 15, 2013, from EBSCO Online Database Business Source Complete. http://search.ebscohost.com/login.aspx?direct=true&db=bth&AN=87734829&site=ehost-live

Walker, C. (2007). Get a lot for a little. *Money (14446219)*, (92), 86. Retrieved September 16, 2007, from EBSCO Online Database Business Source Premier. http://search.ebscohost.com/login.aspx?direct=true&db=buh&AN=25890106&site=ehost-live

Wigan, D. (2013). Convertible bonds: Investors seek convertible cover from rate rises. *Euromoney, 43*(534), 38. Retrieved November 15, 2013, from EBSCO Online Database Business Source Complete. http://search.ebscohost.com/login.aspx?direct=true&db=bth&AN=92025076&site=ehost-live

Suggested Reading

Daves, P., & Ehrhardt, M. (2007). Convertible securities, employee stock options and the cost of equity. *Financial*

Review, 42(2), 267-288. Retrieved September 16, 2007, from EBSCO Online Database Business Source Premier. http://search.ebscohost.com/login.aspx?direct=true&db=buh&AN=25276408&site=ehost-live

Koh, P. (2007). Convertibles' Atlantic drift. *Euromoney, 38*(454), 44-44. Retrieved September 16, 2007, from EBSCO Online Database Business Source Premier. http://search.ebscohost.com/login.aspx?direct=true&db=buh&AN= 24291287&site=ehost-live

Essay by Nancy Devenger

Nancy Devenger holds a BS degree from the University of New Hampshire and a Masters Degree in Health Policy from Dartmouth College's Center for the Evaluative and Clinical Sciences. Nancy began her career in health care as a registered nurse for many years. Since earning her undergraduate degree in Business, Nancy has worked in private medical practice, home health, consulting, and most currently as Director of Ambulatory Operations for a large Academic Medical Center. Her operational experience as a business manager in private medical practice and for the last decade in a tertiary medical center have allowed Nancy broad insight into both private and academic business endeavors.

Swaps

Table of Contents

Abstract

Overview
- Interest Rate Swaps
- Bond Swaps
- Municipal Bonds
- Regulation of Municipal Bonds
- Reasons for Bond Swaps
- International Organizations in the Derivatives Arena

Further Insights
- Risk Management & Analysts' Responsibilities
- The Sarbanes-Oxley Act
- Enterprise Risk Management

Conclusion

Terms & Concepts

Bibliography

Suggested Reading

Abstract

This article examines the swaps market including tax rate swaps, bond swaps, and other derivatives swaps. The origin of swaps is reviewed along with the various uses of securities swaps. The organizations involved in regulating and prompting swaps and the various roles they fulfill are explained. The applications and results of bond swaps are also reviewed along with examples of the types of organizations that have used bond swaps and the motivations behind these practices. Issues with regulating swaps and managing the swaps outcome for investors in light of the 2008-2009 economic crisis are also reviewed.

Overview

In 2009 a survey conducted by the International Swaps and Derivatives Association (ISDA), found that 94 percent of the largest 500 companies in the world are using derivative instruments to manage and hedge their business and financial risks ("Over 94%," 2009). In addition, a large number of American companies use exchange-traded and over-the-counter derivatives to manage various risks. A review of derivatives use reported by the Dow Jones Industrial Average companies shows all 30 of the companies reported using interest-rate and exchange-rate derivatives while 23 of the 30 companies stated they used commodities derivatives and 21 companies mentioned their use of other derivatives ("Use of OTC Derivatives," 2009).

The value of derivatives, which include forward contracts, futures, and options, are determined by the value and the risk related to their underlying assets, which could include stocks, bonds, and even mortgages. The derivatives market, or swaps market, began in 1976 and by 2007 the notational value of the market was over three hundred trillion dollars (Hodgson, 2009). A swap is a privately negotiated agreement between two parties to exchange cash flows at specified payment dates during the agreed-upon life of the contract.

Interest Rate Swaps

An interest rate swap is an agreement to exchange interest rate cash flows, calculated on a notional principal amount, at specified payment dates ("Product Descriptions," 2009). Interest rate swaps first appeared in 1981, and very quickly they became widely used (Stewart & Trussel, 2006). In an interest rate swap each party's payment obligation is computed using a different interest rate and the notional principal is never exchanged ("Product Descriptions," 2009). The principal in an interest rate swap is called notational because it is the basis for calculating the interest and the principal is not exchanged at the end of the agreement. Thus, the principal is not at risk (Brown & Smith, 1993).

A "plain vanilla" swap typically refers to a generic interest rate swap in which one party pays a fixed rate and one party pays a floating rate. The London Interbank-Offered Rate LIBOR), the interest rate paid on interbank deposits in international money markets, is commonly used as a benchmark for short-term interest rates and as the floating rate on an interest rate swap ("Product Descriptions," 2009). Most swap market makers tend to be either commercial or investment banks (Brown & Smith, 1993).

Interest rate swaps generally have periodic review dates written into the agreement and often at the time of review, if the fixed rate exceeds the floating rate, then the party with the fixed rate of interest pays the other party the difference between the two rates. The payment may be calculated by the rate being multiplied by the notional amount for the specified interval of time that has passed. If, on the other hand, the floating rate exceeds the fixed rate, the party with the floating rate pays the other party the difference (Curley & Fella, 2009).

In the contemporary mortgage market mortgages are often connected to asset-backed securities. This securitization process uses the expected future payments from mortgages to support the value of securities that are sold to investors. These investors then have the right to portions of those future payments. The investor then assumes a portion of the risk that borrowers will not pay the mortgages and may default on loans (Gerding, 2009). In the case of mortgages backed by derivatives, any fluctuation in the expected cash flow stream of payments by borrowers can impact the profitability of the securities. Massive failure to repay home loans (as seen in 2008-2009) will of course affect the value of the securities. However, early repayment or refinancing of home loans at lower rates than what were being paid when the securities were issued can also negatively impact the future derived cash stream (Cortes, 2006).

Credit Rating Agencies (CRAs) are companies that grade securities and apply a credit rating based on an assessment based on the likelihood that a debt will be repaid. In the 1960s, CRAs started charging fees to debt issuers for rating their securities. The three largest CRAs are Standard & Poor's (S&P), Moody's Investors Service, and Fitch. Rating credit is an inherently subjective process which requires sound professional judgment. Credit rating professionals rely on vast amounts of quantitative and qualitative data. But a credit rating is only as sound as the research that goes into the rating and the qualifications and integrity of the raters (Coffee, 2009; Rom, 2009).

Bond Swaps

Investors swap bonds by selling one bond or set of bonds and buying another bond or set of bonds with the proceeds of the sale. Bond swapping can help investors improve the quality of their investment portfolio and potentially increase their total return on investment. As economic conditions change, investors may be able to obtain a higher rate of interest on the bonds they hold and change their tax liability when tax laws change. Bond issuers swap bonds as a process of issuing a new bond designed to replace an existing outstanding bond. The results of the swap can change the long term debt position of the issuer and in many cases also provide favorable terms for the investors (Kruger, 2000; "Bond Swapping," 2004).

Municipal Bonds

Since the 1970s local governments have relied on bonds to finance capital building projects including roads, schools, government buildings, and other urban economic development projects. During these 40 years the municipal bond market has grown in value to over $2 trillion. In 1982, Congress passed laws that required that municipal bonds be issued in a registered form in order to retain their tax-exempt status (Hildreth & Zorn, 2005).

Municipal bonds generally pay a specified amount of interest (usually semiannually) and return the principal to the investor on a specific maturity date. One key reason individual investors buy municipal bonds is the tax benefits; interest on the vast majority of municipal bonds is free of federal income tax, and if an investor lives in the state or city issuing the bond, they may also be exempt from state or city taxes on their interest income.

There are two common types of municipal bonds:

- General Obligation Bonds
- Revenue Bonds

General Obligation Bonds are issued by states, cities or counties which are backed by the full faith and credit of the government entity issuing the bonds. Revenue Bonds are backed solely by fees or other revenue generated or collected by a specific facility such as a toll bridge or road. Revenue bonds are not, however, backed by the full faith and credit of the government entity issuing the bonds. The creditworthiness of revenue bonds is determined by and depends on the financial success of the specific project they are issued to fund. Very few municipal bonds have gone into default, but defaults certainly can occur. Defaults tend to be higher for Revenue bonds than for General Obligation bonds, especially those that are used to fund private-use projects such as nursing homes, hospitals or toll roads ("Municipal Bonds," 2009).

Regulation of Municipal Bonds

The Municipal Securities Rulemaking Board (MSRB) makes rules regulating dealers who trade in municipal bonds, municipal notes, and other municipal securities ("Welcome to the MSRB," 2009). The MSRB was established by the United States Congress in 1975 to develop rules for regulating securities firms and banks involved in underwriting, trading, and selling municipal securities. The Board is composed of members from the municipal securities dealer community and the public and is subject to oversight by the Securities and Exchange Commission (SEC). The Board sets rules for:

- Professional qualification standards;
- Fair practice;

- Recordkeeping;
- Confirmation, clearance, and settlement of transactions;
- The scope and frequency of compliance examinations; and
- The nature of securities quotations ("About the MSRB," 2009).

Activities of securities dealers that sell municipal bonds are also subject to the rules set by the Financial Industry Regulatory Authority (FINRA) which mounted a comprehensive analysis of retail sales practices in the municipal securities market and has worked to promote investor protection. FINRA has also examined potential conflicts of interest, disclosure practices, and marketing methods of firms underwriting municipal securities involving swaps and derivatives ("FINRA Takes," 2009).

Reasons for Bond Swaps

Bond swaps occur for a variety of reasons. Issuing organizations including national governments, municipal and state governments as well as private issuers have a long history of bond swaps.

Home finance companies, especially those in the subprime loan market have needed to recapitalize and raise funds to pay existing note holders and to have funds to support the lending process. Bond swaps have helped such companies stay solvent during downturns (Hochstein, 1999). In other cases lending companies have made swaps in order to raise capital to expanding into new markets ("HKMC," 2000).

States, municipal governments, and specialized public organizations such as a turnpike authority have relied on bond swaps to control interest payments and consolidate previous bond issues into new bonds (Braun, 2003; Albanese, 2004; "BAA's," 2008). In addition, several national governments have also relied on bond swaps to control national debt, bolster currency, or improve their credit rating ("Bulgaria," 2002; "Lebanon," 2003; "Dominican Republic," 2005; " Philippines," 2006; "Uruguay," 2008).

International Organizations in the Derivatives Arena

The International Swaps and Derivatives Association (ISDA) represents participants in the privately negotiated derivatives industry. Founded in 1985, the ISDA has over 800 member institutions from 58 countries. The ISDA has worked to identify and reduce the sources of risk in the derivatives and risk management business and has developed the ISDA Master Agreement. The Master Agreement provides a framework for transactions in the over the counter (OTC) derivatives markets ("About ISDA," 2009).

The Securities Industry and Financial Markets Association (SIFMA) represents the interests of participants in the global financial markets on regulatory and legislative issues. Members include international securities firms, registered broker-dealers in the United States as well as asset managers ("The SIFMA Organization," 2009). SIFMA has supported the creation a central authority with oversight in all markets and of all systemically important market participants, the use of clearing houses for standardized transactions, and reporting through data repositories for all other OTC derivative transactions ("Over-the-Counter Derivatives," 2009).

The London Investment Banking Association (LIBA) is the primary trade association in the United Kingdom for companies and organizations that are involved in investment banking and wholesale securities. LIBA works with other trade associations that represent other aspects of the financial services industry, especially on issues that affect all of the participants and where joint activity is an efficient and effective use of resources ("About LIBA," 2009). LIBA is currently addressing issues of accounting, compliance, electronic commerce, financial regulation, and financial crime ("Current Issues," 2009).

Further Insights

Risk Management & Analysts' Responsibilities

Financial securities provide a means for individuals, investment banks, mutual funds, or retirement funds to invest money and to grow the value of their funds. Securities facilitate the process of attracting investors by providing an investment mechanism that is openly and publicly scrutinized by securities analysts and other investors. As the economic downturn of 2008 went from being a downturn to a near catastrophe it was apparent that the scrutiny of securities was not as rigid and comprehensive as it should have been (Bagtas, 2008). There is no doubt that many investment strategies were weak and that many investment analyses were wrong. Much of the economic analyses provided by industry analysts may have been compelling at one point but it became obvious that there was a lack of accuracy and perhaps even a lack of integrity (Savage & Gregory, 2007).

The complexity of global markets, technology innovation, economic interconnectedness and the volume of information necessary to analyze investment alternatives and make investment decisions have all increased over the last twenty years. The interrelationships between all of these aspects sometimes make it difficult to determine the impact that potential changes will have on investment strategies (Freeman, 2009; Freda, Arn, & Gatlin-Watts, 1999).

Recently, the financial industry's computer-based risk models have enabled financial institutions and securities firms to bring more complex derivatives products to investors. However, during the 2008-2009 economic downturn the massive failure of these models led to huge losses for investors and raised questions about how these products were being regulated (Coffee, 2009; Gerding, 2009).

The reliance on computer-supported analytical models used by many analysts quickly became criticized as the economic crisis worsened. Many of the analysts that were using the models and the firms they worked for also faced massive criticism. Many investors and observers contended that there were errors in the assumptions on which the models were built (Segerstrom, 2009). As a result of the heightened controversy, swaps and derivatives in general have come under scrutiny on many fronts. The state government of Massachusetts, for example, is considering limiting the use of swaps by bonding authorities in the state including the Massachusetts Turnpike Authority (Kaske, 2009).

The Sarbanes-Oxley Act

When Enron and WorldCom collapsed, several investment funds and the retirement funds of thousands of individuals lost value. Participants in retirement funds were outraged and angry with the people managing their retirement funds (Minow & Hodgson, 2007). One of many issues surrounding the massive financial collapses of Enron and WorldCom was the accuracy and reliability of internal audits. These audits are provided to the board of directors and the stockholders as accurate depictions of the financial health and condition of a publicly traded company. Reports are also filed with the SEC as a matter of public record.

The Sarbanes-Oxley Act of 2002 was a significant step in the regulation of publicly traded companies and was intended to help protect investors by requiring more stringent controls on corporate financial reporting and disclosures. The act established the Public Company Accounting Oversight Board (PCAOB) as a private-sector non-profit organization that is charged with overseeing the audits of public traded companies. These companies are regulated by numerous securities laws and are required to file periodic reports with the SEC.

The Sarbanes-Oxley Act addressed the reliability and independence of audits and required that any and all documentation regarding financial statements be preserved. The act also holds executive officers and boards of directors more accountable for the accuracy of financial reports and prescribes rather severe criminal penalties for false or misleading reports (Shear, 2006).

Enterprise Risk Management

Enterprise Risk Management (ERM) analytical models are designed to encompass both external and internal risks which include all of the investment mechanisms that a financial investment firm, bank, or other company holds (Muzzy, 2008). To perform a comprehensive and in-depth risk analysis of investments requires obtaining data from numerous sources as well as testing the integrity and accuracy of that data (Vlasenko & Kozlov, 2009). ERM enables corporate executives to aggregate, prioritize, and effectively manage risks while enabling business-unit managers to improve decision making in operations and product management (Kocourek & Newfrock, 2006).

The 2008 economic downturn caught many corporate executives working with analytical models that assumed that the housing market would not decline so drastically or on such a widespread basis (Korolov, 2009). Although it was clear that most risk managers had also not previously seen the convergence of negative economic trends occur so quickly or across so many sectors simultaneously, it became clear that the assumptions about risk and the analytical models to analyze risk had not undergone stringent enough testing. (Morgan, 2009). As a result of the many errors in risk analysis prior to the 2008-2009 economic crisis investment advisors, institutional investors, and credit rating agencies are adding to the pressure for companies to develop ERM systems and disclose their risks (Karlin, 2007).

Conclusion

The swaps market has many facets, with various financial securities that can be swapped including bonds, futures, options, and interest rate agreements. Each of these financial securities is a world in and of itself. Investors rely on financial advisors to help guide their investment decisions which means that financial advisors either must be well versed in a variety of securities or specialize in a particular area.

The complexities of the swap market combined with the inter-relationships of a wide arena of swappable securities, all in an interconnected global economy means that laws, regulations, practices, and ethics need to address how the performance of one market or one security can impact other markets or other securities. Financial securities provide both a means of creating and maintaining wealth as well as making capital available to organizations that can contribute to economic growth.

Be it the dotcom boom and bust of the 1990s, or the real estate market crash of the new millennium, it is clear that investors need to be cautious of their decisions and perhaps even more cautious of the advice they take or leave from the battalions of financial advisors that are eager to serve them.

Terms & Concepts

Derivative: A financial investment product, whose value is derived from an underlying security and can include interest rate swaps, caps, as well as many other types of variable rate investment mechanism.

Enterprise Risk Management: A data intensive process that measures all of a company's risks including financial risks, investment oriented risks, operations based risks, and market risks, as well as legal and regulatory risks for all of the locations which a company operates or invests (Peterson, 2006).

Futures: An arrangement in which two parties agree to buy and sell the value of a security or a commodity at an agreed upon date or period in the future.

London Inter-Bank Offered Rate (LIBOR): A benchmark interest rate upon which many transactions are based and obligations of parties to such transactions are typically expressed as a spread to LIBOR ("Glossary of Municipal Securities Terms," 2009).

Options: An agreement in which two parties agree to buy and sell a security or a commodity at an agreed upon price at an agreed upon date or period in the future.

Swaps: A sale of a security and the simultaneous purchase of another security for purposes of enhancing the investor's holdings. The swap may be used to achieve desired tax results, to gain income or principal, or to alter various features of a bond portfolio ("Glossary of Municipal Securities Terms," 2009).

Bibliography

About ISDA. (2009). The International Swaps and Derivatives Association. Accessed September 1, 2009. http://www.isda.org/index.html

About LIBA. (2009). The London Investment Banking Association. Accessed September 1, 2009. http://www.liba.org.uk/

About the MSRB. (2009). The Municipal Securities Rulemaking Board. Accessed September 7, 2009. http://www.msrb.org/msrb1/whatsnew/default.asp

Albanese, E. (2004). Colorado RTD Waiting for the right time to swap $132M. Bond Buyer, 347(31794), 28-28. Retrieved September 6, 2009, from EBSCO online database, Business Source Premier. http://search.ebscohost.com/login.aspx?direct=true&db=buh&AN=11854905&site=ehost-live

BAA's bond swap is cleared for take-off as ABI signs on. (2008, July 18). *Euroweek,* (Issue 1063). 50. Retrieved September 6, 2009, from EBSCO online database, Business Source Premier. http://search.ebscohost.com/login.aspx?direct=true&db=buh&AN=34638815&site=ehost-live

Bagtas, M. (2008). Who's to blame for the U.S. subprime mortgage meltdown? *Ateneo Law Journal, 53*(3), 844-853. Retrieved September 2, 2009, from EBSCO online database, Academic Search Complete http://search.ebscohost.com/login.aspx?direct=true&db=a9h&AN=43097053&site=ehost-live

Barlas, S. (2013). Cross-border swaps proposals worry business groups. *Strategic Finance, 95*(10), 23. Retrieved November 15, 2013, from EBSCO Online Database Business Source Complete. http://search.ebscohost.com/login.aspx?direct=true&db=bth&AN=90612622&site=ehost-live

Bond Swapping an investor's guide: Techniques to lower your taxes and improve the quality of your portfolio. (2004). Retrieved September 1, 2009, from The Securities Industry and Financial Markets. http://www.sifma.org/services/publications/pdf/BondSwapping1004.pdf

Braun, M. (2003). N.J. treasurer says state may utilize school-bond swaps for other projects. *Bond Buyer, 344*(31637), 5. Retrieved September 6, 2009, from EBSCO online database, Business Source Premier. http://search.ebscohost.com/login.aspx?direct=true&db=buh&AN=9893107&site=ehost-live

Brown, K., & Smith, D. (1993). Default risk and innovations in the design of interest rate swaps. *FM: The Journal of the Financial Management Association, 22*(2), 94. Retrieved September 3, 2009, from EBSCO online database, Business Source Premier. http://search.ebscohost.com/login.aspx?direct=true&db=buh&AN=9403082325&site=ehost-live

Bulgaria completes $759m second Brady swap via JP Morgan and Citi, saving $242m. (2002, September 27). *Euroweek,* (Issue 772). 16. Retrieved September 6, 2009, from EBSCO online database, Business Source Premier. http://search.ebscohost.com/login.aspx?direct=true&db=buh&AN=7538687&site=ehost-live

Chernenko, S., & Faulkender, M. (2011). The two sides of derivatives usage: hedging and speculating with interest rate swaps. *Journal of Financial & Quantitative Analysis, 46*(6), 1727-1754. Retrieved November 15, 2013, from EBSCO Online Database Business Source Complete. http://search.ebscohost.com/login.aspx?direct=true&db=bth&AN=71818599&site=ehost-live

Coffee Jr, J. (2009). What went wrong? An initial inquiry into the causes of the 2008 financial crisis. *Journal of Corporate Law Studies, 9*(1), 1-22. Retrieved September 2, 2009, from EBSCO online database, Academic Search Complete. http://search.ebscohost.com/login.aspx?direct=true&db=a9h&AN=38606869&site=ehost-live

Cortes, F. (2006). Understanding the term structure of swap spreads. *Bank of England Quarterly Bulletin, 46*(1), 45-56. Retrieved August 31, 2009, from EBSCO online database, Business Source Premier. http://search.ebscohost.com/login.aspx?direct=true&db=buh&AN=20227743&site=ehost-live

Curley, S., & Fella, E. (2009). Where to hide? How valuation of derivatives haunts the courts — even after BAPCPA. *American Bankruptcy Law Journal, 83*(2), 297-323. Retrieved September 1, 2009, from EBSCO online database, Business Source Premier. http://search.ebscohost.

com/login.aspx?direct=true&db=buh&AN=42833751&site=ehost-live

Current Issues. (2009). The London Investment Banking Association. Accessed September 1, 2009 http://www.liba.org.uk/Dominican Republic offers bond swap without haircut. (2005, April 22). *Euroweek,* (Issue 900). 26-26. Retrieved September 6, 2009, from EBSCO online database, Business Source Premier. http://search.ebscohost.com/login.aspx?direct=true&db=buh&AN=17016414&site=ehost-live

FINRA takes sweeping action to protect muni bond investors. (2009). The Financial Industry Regulatory Authority. Accessed September 7, 2009. http://www.finra.org/Newsroom/NewsReleases/2009/P119064

Freda, G., Arn, J., & Gatlin-Watts, R. (1999). Adapting to the speed of change. *Industrial Management, 41*(6), 31. Retrieved September 2, 2009, from EBSCO online database, Business Source Premier. http://search.ebscohost.com/login.aspx?direct=true&db=bth&AN=2772106&site=ehost-live

Freeman, L. (2009). Who's guarding the gate? Credit-rating agency liability as control person in the subprime credit crisis. *Vermont Law Review, 33*(3), 585-619. Retrieved September 2, 2009, from EBSCO online database, Academic Search Complete. http://search.ebscohost.com/login.aspx?direct=true&db=a9h&AN=43308037&site=ehost-live

Gerding, E. (2009). Code, crash, and open source: The outsourcing of financial regulation to risk models and the global financial crisis. *Washington Law Review, 84*(2), 127-198. Retrieved September 1, 2009, from EBSCO online database, Academic Search Complete. http://search.ebscohost.com/login.aspx?direct=true&db=a9h&AN=43248135&site=ehost-live

Glossary of Municipal Securities Terms. (2009). The Municipal Securities Rulemaking Board. Accessed September 7, 2009. http://www.msrb.org/msrb1/glossary/glossary%5fdb.asp?sel=s

HKMC in mortgage/bond swap. (2000, June 2). *Euroweek,* Issue 655, 8-8. Retrieved September 6, 2009, from EBSCO online database, Business Source Premier. http://search.ebscohost.com/login.aspx?direct=true&db=buh&AN=3202248&site=ehost-live

Hildreth, W., & Zorn, C. (2005, December 2). The evolution of the state and local government municipal debt market over the past quarter century. *Public Budgeting & Finance, 25,* 127-153. Retrieved September 7, 2009, from EBSCO online database, Business Source Premier. http://search.ebscohost.com/login.aspx?direct=true&db=buh&AN=18943868&site=ehost-live

Hochstein, M. (1999). Ga. lender, facing default, plans to offer a bond swap. *American Banker, 164*(248), 6. Retrieved September 6, 2009, from EBSCO online database, Business Source Premier. http://search.ebscohost.com/login.aspx?direct=true&db=buh&AN=2636371&site=ehost-live

Hodgson, R. (2009). The birth of the swap. *Financial Analysts Journal, 65*(3), 1-4. Retrieved September 1, 2009, from EBSCO online database, Business Source Premier. http://search.ebscohost.com/login.aspx?direct=true&db=buh&AN=38703192&site=ehost-live

Karlin, B. (2007). Sweating out the ERMs. *Treasury & Risk,* (Dec/Jan), 15. Retrieved September 2, 2009, from EBSCO online database, Business Source Premier. http://search.ebscohost.com/login.aspx?direct=true&db=buh&AN=28144191&site=ehost-live

Kaske, M. (2009). Massachusetts mulls curbs on swaps. (cover story). *Bond Buyer, 369*(33155), 1-4. Retrieved August 31, 2009, from EBSCO online database, Business Source Premier. http://search.ebscohost.com/login.aspx?direct=true&db=buh&AN=43515641&site=ehost-live

Kocourek, P., & Newfrock, J. (2006). Are boards worrying about the wrong risks? *Corporate Board, 27*(157), 6-11. Retrieved September 3, 2009, from EBSCO online database, Business Source Premier. http://search.ebscohost.com/login.aspx?direct=true&db=buh&AN=19887261&site=ehost-live

Korolov, M. (2009). Enterprise risk management: Getting holistic. (cover story). *Securities Industry News, 21*(15), 1-6. Retrieved September 2, 2009, from EBSCO online database, Business Source Premier. http://search.ebscohost.com/login.aspx?direct=true&db=buh&AN=43249547&site=ehost-live

Kruger, D. (2000). Bond Swap. *Forbes, 166*(13), 358-358. Retrieved September 6, 2009, from EBSCO online database, Academic Search Complete. http://search.ebscohost.com/login.aspx?direct=true&db=a9h&AN=3717090&site=ehost-live

Lebanon plans $1bn-$2bn bond swap to cut redemption hump in 2005-2006. (cover story). (2003). *Euroweek,* (Issue 829) 1-2. Retrieved September 6, 2009, from EBSCO online database, Business Source Premier. http://search.ebscohost.com/login.aspx?direct=true&db=buh&AN=11521327&site=ehost-live

Minow, N., & Hodgson, P. (2007). Shareholder activism and the eclipse of the public corporation. *Corporate Board, 28*(164), 1-5. Retrieved September 2, 2009, from EBSCO online database, Business Source Premier. http://search.ebscohost.com/login.aspx?direct=true&db=bth&AN=24876959&site=ehost-live

Morgan, J. (2009, May 27). Firms adjust to new world of risk. *Investment Management Weekly,* Retrieved September 2, 2009, from EBSCO online database, Business Source Premier. http://search.ebscohost.com/login.aspx?direct=true&db=buh&AN=40730215&site=ehost-live

Municipal Bonds — Staying on the safe side of the street in rough times. (2009). The Financial Industry Regulatory Authority. Accessed September 7, 2009. http://www.finra.org/Investors/ProtectYourself/InvestorAlerts/Bonds/P1188923

Muzzy, L. (2008). Approaching Enterprise Risk Management. *Financial Executive, 24*(8), 59-61. Retrieved September 2, 2009, from EBSCO online database, Business Source Premier. http://search.ebscohost.com/login.aspx?direct=true&db=buh&AN=34736453&site=ehost-live

Over 94% of the world's largest companies use derivatives to help manage their risks, according to ISDA survey. (2009). The International Swaps and Derivatives Association. Accessed September 1, 2009. http://www.isda.org/press/press042309der.pdf

Over-the-counter derivatives, (2009). The Securities Industry and Financial Markets. Accessed September 1, 2009. http://www.sifma.org/legislative/OTC/otc-derivatives.aspx?ID=11824

Peterson, J. (2006). Ready for ERM. (cover story). *ABA Banking Journal, 98*(1), 19-23. Retrieved September 3, 2009, from EBSCO online database, Business Source Premier. http://search.ebscohost.com/login.aspx?direct=true&db=buh&AN=19357897&site=ehost-live

Philippines begins 10 year peso bond swap. (2006, August 18). *Euroweek,* (Issue 967, Special Section).1-6. Retrieved September 6, 2009, from EBSCO online database, Business Source Premier. http://search.ebscohost.com/login.aspx?direct=true&db=buh&AN=22354919&site=ehost-live

Product descriptions and Frequently Asked Questions. (2009). The International Swaps and Derivatives Association. Accessed September 1, 2009. http://www.isda.org/educat/faqs.html#2

Rom, M. (2009). The credit rating agencies and the subprime mess: Greedy, ignorant, and stressed? *Public Administration Review, 69*(4), 640-650. Retrieved September 2, 2009, from EBSCO online database, Business Source Premier. http://search.ebscohost.com/login.aspx?direct=true&db=buh&AN=42960191&site=ehost-live

Saretto, A., & Tookes, H.E. (2013). Corporate leverage, debt maturity, and credit supply: the role of credit default swaps. *Review of Financial Studies, 26*(5), 1190-1247. Retrieved November 15, 2013, from EBSCO Online Database Business Source Complete. http://search.ebscohost.com/login.aspx?direct=true&db=bth&AN=87109278&site=ehost-live

Savage, S., & Gregory, K. (2007). It's fundamental. *Financial Planning, 37*(11), 151-152. Retrieved September 2, 2009, from EBSCO online database, Business Source Premier. http://search.ebscohost.com/login.aspx?direct=true&db=buh&AN=27350413&site=ehost-live

Segerstrom, J. (2009). Are financial models really to blame? *Bank Accounting & Finance (08943958), 22*(5), 39-42. Retrieved September 2, 2009, from EBSCO online database, Business Source Premier. http://search.ebscohost.com/login.aspx?direct=true&db=buh&AN=43610023&site=ehost-live

Shear, W. (2006). Sarbanes-Oxley Act: Consideration of key principles needed in addressing implementation for smaller public companies. Retrieved September 5, 2009, from the United States Government Accountability Office. http://www.gao.gov/new.items/d06361.pdf

Stewart, L., & Trussel, J. (2006). The use of interest rate swaps by nonprofit organizations: evidence from nonprofit health care providers. *Journal of Health Care Finance, 33*(2), 6-22. Retrieved September 3, 2009, from EBSCO online database, Business Source Premier. http://search.ebscohost.com/login.aspx?direct=true&db=buh&AN=23606132&site=ehost-live

The SIFMA Organization. (2009). The securities industry and financial markets. Accessed September 1, 2009. http://www.sifma.org/about

Uruguay to swap bonds up to $802m. (2008, June 27). *Euroweek,* (1060). 16-16. Retrieved September 6, 2009, from EBSCO online database, Business Source Premier. http://search.ebscohost.com/login.aspx?direct=true&db=buh&AN=33276363&site=ehost-live

Use of OTC derivatives by American companies. (2009). The Securities Industry and Financial Markets. Accessed September 1, 2009. http://www.sifma.org/uploadedFiles/Government%5fAffairs/OTC/Use%20of%20OTC%20Derivatives%20by%20American%20Companies%20June%202009(1).pdf

Vlasenko, O., & Kozlov, S. (2009). Choosing the risk curve type. *Technological & Economic Development of Economy, 15*(2), 341-351. Retrieved September 2, 2009, from EBSCO online database, Business Source Premier. http://search.ebscohost.com/login.aspx?direct=true&db=buh&AN=43181065&site=ehost-live

Watson III, J. (2009). Industry faces more uncertainty than ever. *On Wall Street, 19*(5), 40-42. Retrieved September 2, 2009, from EBSCO online database, Business Source Premier. http://search.ebscohost.com/login.aspx?direct=true&db=buh&AN=41129061&site=ehost-live

Welcome to the MSRB. (2009). The Municipal Securities Rulemaking Board. Accessed September 7, 2009. http://www.msrb.org/msrb1/

Suggested Reading

Armitage, S. (1996). The cost of bank loans in relation to bonds swapped into a floating rate. *European Financial Management, 2*(3), 311. Retrieved September 3, 2009, from EBSCO online database, Business Source Premier. http://search.ebscohost.com/login.aspx?direct=true&db=buh&AN=5319506&site=ehost-live

Barlas, S. (2009). Regulation of credit default swaps. *Strategic Finance, 90*(9), 24-61. Retrieved September 1, 2009, from EBSCO online database, Business Source Premier. http://search.ebscohost.com/login.aspx?direct=true&db=buh&AN=36793846&site=ehost-live

Baviera, R. (2006). Bond market model. *International Journal of Theoretical & Applied Finance, 9*(4), 577-596. Retrieved September 3, 2009, from EBSCO online database, Business Source Premier. http://search.ebscohost.com/login.aspx?direct=true&db=buh&AN=21356736&site=ehost-live

Bee, M. (2004). Modelling credit default swap spreads by means of normal mixtures and copulas. *Applied Mathematical Finance, 11*(2), 125-146. Retrieved September 1, 2009, from EBSCO online database, Business Source Premier. http://search.ebscohost.com/login.aspx?direct=true&db=buh&AN=13307693&site=ehost-live

Betzold, N., & Berg, R. (1995). Is 'bond-swap' logic reality or wishful thinking? ABA *Banking Journal, 87*(12), 49. Retrieved September 3, 2009, from EBSCO online database, Business Source Premier. http://search.ebscohost.com/login.aspx?direct=true&db=buh&AN=9512294237&site=ehost-live

Bierwag, G., & Kaufman, G. (1991). Expected bond returns and duration: A general model. *Financial Analysts Journal, 47*(1), 83-84. Retrieved September 3, 2009, from EBSCO online database, Business Source Premier. http://search.ebscohost.com/login.aspx?direct=true&db=buh&AN=7026727&site=ehost-live

Brooks, L. (1984). Stock-bond swaps in regulated utilities. *Financial Management (1972), 13*(3), 5-10. Retrieved September 3, 2009, from EBSCO online database, Business Source Premier. http://search.ebscohost.com/login.aspx?direct=true&db=buh&AN=5029251&site=ehost-live

Bryan, S., & Lilien, S. (2008). The case of interest rate swaps and questions for the pozen committee. *CPA Journal, 78*(6), 26-31. Retrieved September 1, 2009, from EBSCO online database, Business Source Premier. http://search.ebscohost.com/login.aspx?direct=true&db=buh&AN=32590270&site=ehost-live

Castagnetti, C. (2004). Estimating the risk premium of swap spreads. Two econometric GARCH-based techniques. *Applied Financial Economics, 14*(2), 93-104. Retrieved September 1, 2009, from EBSCO online database, Business Source Premier. http://search.ebscohost.com/login.aspx?direct=true&db=buh&AN=11900862&site=ehost-live

Choudhry, M. (2006). An alternative bond relative value measure: Determining a fair value of the swap spread using Libor and GC repo rates. *Journal of Asset Management, 7*(1), 17-21. Retrieved September 3, 2009, from EBSCO online database, Business Source Premier. http://search.ebscohost.com/login.aspx?direct=true&db=buh&AN=21466926&site=ehost-live

Colabella, P., Fitzsimons, A., & Shoaf, V. (2009). SEC sets stage for credit default swap oversight. *Bank Accounting & Finance (08943958), 22*(4), 45-52. Retrieved September 1, 2009, from EBSCO online database, Business Source Premier. http://search.ebscohost.com/login.aspx?direct=true&db=buh&AN=43158010&site=ehost-live

Collin-Dufresne, P., & Solnik, B. (2001). On the term structure of default premia in the swap and LIBOR markets. *Journal of Finance, 56*(3), 1095-1115. Retrieved August 31, 2009, from EBSCO online database, Business Source Premier. http://search.ebscohost.com/login.aspx?direct=true&db=buh&AN=4673626&site=ehost-live

Daniels, K., & Jensen, M. (2005). The effect of credit ratings on credit default swap spreads and credit spreads. *Journal of Fixed Income, 15*(3), 16-33. Retrieved September 3,

2009, from EBSCO online database, Business Source Premier. http://search.ebscohost.com/login.aspx?direct=true&db=buh&AN=19482099&site=ehost-live

Duffie, D. (1999). Credit swap valuation. *Financial Analysts Journal, 55*(1), 73. Retrieved September 3, 2009, from EBSCO online database, Business Source Premier. http://search.ebscohost.com/login.aspx?direct=true&db=buh&AN=1590633&site=ehost-live

Dunis, C., & Morrison, V. (2007). The economic value of advanced time series methods for modelling and trading 10-year government bonds. *European Journal of Finance, 13*(4), 333-352. Retrieved September 7, 2009, from EBSCO online database, Business Source Premier. http://search.ebscohost.com/login.aspx?direct=true&db=buh&AN=25390269&site=ehost-live

Fan, R., Gupta, A., & Ritchken, P. (2007). On pricing and hedging in the swaption market: How many factors, really? *Journal of Derivatives, 15*(1), 9-33. Retrieved September 1, 2009, from EBSCO online database, Business Source Premier. http://search.ebscohost.com/login.aspx?direct=true&db=buh&AN=26590064&site=ehost-live

Finnerty, J. (2001). Premium debt swaps, tax-timing arbitrage, and debt service parity . *Journal of Applied Finance, 11*(1), 17. Retrieved September 3, 2009, from EBSCO online database, Business Source Premier. http://search.ebscohost.com/login.aspx?direct=true&db=buh&AN=5899633&site=ehost-live

Fung, H., Sierra, G., Yau, J., & Zhang, G. (2008). Are the U.S. stock market and credit default swap market related? Evidence from the CDX indices. *Journal of Alternative Investments, 11*(1), 43-61. Retrieved September 1, 2009, from EBSCO online database, Business Source Premier. http://search.ebscohost.com/login.aspx?direct=true&db=buh&AN=33119596&site=ehost-live

Gabaldon, T. (2009). Financial federalism and the short, happy life of municipal securities regulation. *Journal of Corporation Law, 34*(3), 739-769. Retrieved September 7, 2009, from EBSCO online database, Business Source Premier. http://search.ebscohost.com/login.aspx?direct=true&db=buh&AN=38703149&site=ehost-live

Goswami, G., & Shrikhande, M. (2007). Economic exposure and currency swaps. *Journal of Applied Finance, 17*(2), 62-71. Retrieved September 1, 2009, from EBSCO online database, Business Source Premier. http://search.ebscohost.com/login.aspx?direct=true&db=buh&AN=32604422&site=ehost-live

Heidari, M., & Wu, L. (2009). A joint framework for consistently pricing interest rates and interest rate derivatives. *Journal of Financial & Quantitative Analysis, 44*(3), 517-550. Retrieved September 1, 2009, from EBSCO online database, Business Source Premier. http://search.ebscohost.com/login.aspx?direct=true&db=buh&AN=43892240&site=ehost-live

Jamshidian, F. (2008). Bivariate support of forward libor and swap rates. *Mathematical Finance, 18*(3), 427-443. Retrieved September 1, 2009, from EBSCO online database, Business Source Premier. http://search.ebscohost.com/login.aspx?direct=true&db=buh&AN=32575071&site=ehost-live

Kim, J. (2007). Can risks be reduced in the derivatives market? Lessons from the deal structure analysis of modern financial engineering debacles. *DePaul Business & Commercial Law Journal, 6*(1), 29-142. Retrieved September 1, 2009, from EBSCO online database, Business Source Premier. http://search.ebscohost.com/login.aspx?direct=true&db=buh&AN=31656608&site=ehost-live

Kim, J. (2008). From vanilla swaps to exotic credit derivatives: How to approach the interpretation of credit events. *Fordham Journal of Corporate & Financial Law, 13*(5), 705-804. Retrieved September 1, 2009, from EBSCO online database, Business Source Premier. http://search.ebscohost.com/login.aspx?direct=true&db=buh&AN=34234186&site=ehost-live

Klein, P. (2004). Interest rate swaps: Reconciliation of models. *Journal of Derivatives, 12*(1), 46-57. Retrieved September 3, 2009, from EBSCO online database, Business Source Premier. http://search.ebscohost.com/login.aspx?direct=true&db=buh&AN=14353069&site=ehost-live

Lingane, P. (2008). Benefits and management of inflation-protected treasury bonds. *Journal of Financial Planning, 21*(9), 60-68. Retrieved September 7, 2009, from EBSCO online database, Business Source Premier. http://search.ebscohost.com/login.aspx?direct=true&db=buh&AN=34262457&site=ehost-live

Meng, L., & Ap Gwilym, O. (2007). The characteristics and evolution of credit default swap trading. *Journal of Derivatives & Hedge Funds, 13*(3), 186-198. Retrieved September 1, 2009, from EBSCO online database, Business Source Premier. http://search.ebscohost.com/login.aspx?direct=true&db=buh&AN=30015176&site=ehost-live

Misra, R., & Tierney, J. (2001). Managing a corporate risk portfolio: Convergence between corporate loans, bonds and default swaps. *Derivatives Use, Trading & Regulation, 7*(3), 231. Retrieved September 3, 2009, from EBSCO online database, Business Source Premier. http://search.ebscohost.com/login.aspx?direct=true&db=buh&AN=6897633&site=ehost-live

O'Brien, T., Schmid Klein, L., & Hilliard, J. (2007). Capital structure swaps and shareholder wealth. *European Financial Management, 13*(5), 979-997. Retrieved September 1, 2009, EBSCO online database, Business Source Premier. http://search.ebscohost.com/login.aspx?direct=true&db=buh&AN=27173450&site=ehost-live

Ollie, E., Kolb-Collier, D., & Clay, S. (2007). Defending A+ how to maintain a high credit rating during a facilities overhaul. *hfm (Healthcare Financial Management), 61*(11), 114-120. Retrieved September 7, 2009, from EBSCO online database, Business Source Premier. Source Premier database. http://search.ebscohost.com/login.aspx?direct=true&db=buh&AN=27494153&site=ehost-live

Robbins, M., & Kim, D. (2003). Do state bond banks have cost advantages for municipal bond issuance? *Public Budgeting & Finance, 23*(3), 92-108. Retrieved September 7, 2009, from EBSCO online database, Business Source Premier. http://search.ebscohost.com/login.aspx?direct=true&db=buh&AN=10582491&site=ehost-live

Wu, T., & Chen, S. (2007). Cross-currency equity swaps in the BGM model. *Journal of Derivatives, 15*(2), 60-76. Retrieved September 1, 2009, from EBSCO online database, Business Source Premier. http://search.ebscohost.com/login.aspx?direct=true&db=buh&AN=27819835&site=ehost-live

---

Essay by Michael Erbschloe, M.A.

Michael Erbschloe is an information technology consultant, educator, and author. He has taught graduate level courses and developed technology-related curriculum for several universities and speaks at conferences and industry events around the world. Michael holds a Masters Degree in Sociology from Kent State University. He has authored hundreds of articles and several books on technology.